What People Are Saying About Tony, Peter and This Book...

"Their writings are a success 'playbook' that will raise the performance of top leaders across the business world."
- RICKY RICHARDSON, PRESIDENT, TGI FRIDAY'S, USA

"Peter Thomas is a master visionary as Tony Jeary is an extraordinary strategist. Together they have collaborated on a book I wish I had twenty years ago. It would have saved a whole heap of trial and error."
- VINCE POSCENTE, NY TIMES BESTSELLING AUTHOR, THE AGE OF SPEED

"I have found Tony's insights to be both practical and helpful."
- JAMES O'CONNOR, PRESIDENT, FORD MOTOR CO.

"I am not only impressed with your coaching skills, but more importantly your genuine commitment to supporting your clients and building a true partnership."
- TOM GRIMM, FORMER PRESIDENT & CEO, SAM'S CLUB

"If you want to learn how to think clearly in evaluating your opportunities, strategize wisely, and execute successfully, then this is the book for you! Lives will be changed by this one."
- DON HUTSON, CO-AUTHOR OF NY TIMES INTERNATIONAL BESTSELLER, THE ONE MINUTE ENTREPRENEUR

"This book shares collective wisdom from a countless number of extremely successful leaders. Tony's passion for helping people learn in an accelerated fashion comes to life on these pages."
- JIM GREENWOOD, PRESIDENT AND CEO, VISIONSOURCE

"Dedicated to advancing serious entrepreneurs growing their organizations... Tony's pro bono contributions have dramatically impacted the success of our entrepreneur students with the content in this work."
- JAY RODGERS, FOUNDER, BIZ OWNERS ED

"Young Entrepreneurs' Organization (YEO) and Entrepreneurs' Organization (EO) would not exist if it weren't for Peter Thomas, first and foremost. Peter's leadership and passion drove a handful of other young entrepreneurs and a few full-time staffers to develop the most comprehensive and respected entrepreneurs peer group in the world. Peter has been a mentor to many."

- MATT MLADENKA, VICE PRESIDENT MARKETING OF
CONSUMER INSIGHT, DIGITAL AND BRANDING

"Peter is 'A Tour De Force' with extraordinary insight as to what is in us all to be the very best that we can be."

- MICHAEL O'BRIAN, PRESIDENT - NAIRBO INVESTMENTS INC.

"This book is a must read for entrepreneurs! Peter Thomas and Tony Jeary provide you with 100 key rules for accelerating success and having a richer life."

- TONY HARTL, FOUNDER OF PLANET TAN, CEO OF PAH
CAPITAL, LLC

"Invest 10 minutes a day reading three short Ground Rules, and in one short month you will re-energize your business."

- DAVID HUMPHREY, FORMER PRESIDENT MASSAGE ENVY

"My life is better because Tony is in it."

- RON LUSK, SERIAL ENTREPRENEUR AND INVESTOR

"Tony Jeary is a phenomenon! I have always been mesmerized at his incredible gifts, skill sets, expertise, and knowledge base in working with and helping clients maximize their potential. He has the unique ability to help any level of Senior Executive, Owner, and Entrepreneur."

- DENNIS WINDSOR, CO-FOUNDER & PRESIDENT AT NERIUM
INTERNATIONAL

"I swear I got more mileage from the money I spent with you than probably any money I've ever spent. I'm still using the tactics years later. Thanks again."

- DAVE LESH, FOUNDER, DALE DENTAL, E.O. MEMBER, DALLAS

"*Business Ground Rules* is the latest edition showcasing Peter's keen ability to remind us all about what it means to truly achieve success in life."

    - ADAM R. KAUFMAN, BILTMORE ADVISORY GROUP,
    FOUNDER UP2

"I had the opportunity to work with Peter at last year's Global Student Entrepreneur Awards. From the moment I met Peter, I knew he was a person of Integrity and Honor. His warmth and generosity of spirit overflows. His exceptional kindness and mentorship is evident in the many successful young faces he interacts with. I am proud to know Peter and look forward to working together more."

    - ADAM SIETZ, AWARD-WINNING ENTERTAINMENT
    PROFESSIONAL & CONSULTANT

"Thanks for challenging all of us into moving from good, to great, to Mastery!"

    - JOHN WRIGHT, SALES MANAGER, MITSUBISHI

"Thinking through all aspects of our strategic planning has been quite helpful moving from strategic to tactical execution… All things remain at rest until energy is applied, and Tony will transfer his energy to you and your team."

    - RAY GREER, CEO, BNSF LOGISTICS

"Peter Thomas knows there is more to success than a job title or bank balance. His passion, enthusiasm, and commitment will infect every aspect of your life."

    - CATHERINE CRIER, AUTHOR OF THE NY TIMES BESTSELLER,
    A DEADLY GAME

"You bring all new meaning to efficiency and effectiveness."

    - JOEL BARKER, FUTURIST AND AUTHOR OF *THE NEW BUSINESS OF PARADIGMS*

"If you want to truly love your life, Peter and Tony will show you how by living with intention."

    - BOB CAMPANA, CAMPANA CAPITAL

"My success in selling deals and inspiring people to commitment to a deal, is a direct result of the lessons I learned from Peter. Whenever I am challenged in motivating or inspiring anyone, I always ask myself, 'What would Peter say?'"
>   - MARK PEERS, RESIDENTIAL DESIGN & CONSTRUCTION,
>   PROJECT MANAGEMENT, SAMOTH CAPITAL CORPORATION

"Tony has always been excellent at helping top leaders develop their communication skills and their personal brands."
>   -TONY BINGHAM, PRESIDENT & CEO, THE AMERICAN SOCIETY
>   FOR TRAINING & DEVELOPMENT

"Whether you are in sales or the CEO of a billion dollar corporation, let Tony Jeary be your personal coach."
>   - MARK VICTOR HANSEN, AUTHOR OF CHICKEN SOUP FOR THE
>   SOUL

"Tony is the best strategist I have seen in action . . . He brings energy, focus, and actionable ideas that impact businesses immediately. Engage Tony today if you want to dramatically drive growth in your company."
>   - ALLAN DZIWOKI, MITSUBISHI ELECTRIC HVAC

"In my experience, it is not often someone promises to meet and exceed my expectations and then actually does so!"
>   - JON MCKILLIP, PRESIDENT,
>   WORLD VENTURES INTERNATIONAL

"Peter's mature, calm advice resonates to all levels of self-improvement, making life's greatest challenges seem more manageable."
>   - BRENT T. BARKER, STRATA CAPITAL GROUP

"This book should be turned into a mandatory college course at all universities across America."
>   - CARSON LYNCH, YOUTH ADVISORY BOARD

". . . invaluable in making our company leaders objectively evaluate the company, and in establishing goals for better performance."
>   - RUSSELL LAUGHLIN, HILLWOOD PROPERTIES, A ROSS PEROT
>   COMPANY

"Tony Jeary has been a mentor of mine for years. *Business Ground Rules* is not just a book, it is a manual for life!"
- RYAN CHAMBERLIN, AUTHOR OF *NOW YOU KNOW*

"Peter Thomas' books have changed the lives of many for the better; I am grateful to be one of the many."
- MARK HORNE

"Tony Jeary is a master... Tony truly does give value and does more than is expected!"
- MIKE ARCANGELO, SANOFI PASTEUR

"Tony Jeary's methods are the most critical and final step in assuring maximum success in any organization, be it the largest corporation or even your household. Without utilizing his methodology, even the best strategy will be sub-optimized!"
- MIKE GADE, CHIEF MARKETING OFFICER, 7-ELEVEN

"Your library of information, ideas, and systems is a real treasure."
- R MORRIS SIMS, CORP. VP, NEW YORK LIFE

"Excellent investment!"
- KEITH CARGILL, PRESIDENT, TEXAS CAPITAL BANK

"You rock!"
- STUART JOHNSON, OWNER, *SUCCESS MAGAZINE*

"Great ideas, great contacts, and great action items."
- CARSON CONANT, EVP, NIGHTINGALE CONANT

"Peter Thomas has given an understanding to how one can continue to succeed while living a happier life."
- FADI E. KHOURY

"You are a true Master. We have seen and worked with the best... the best investment we have made in years... Thank you for coaching!"
- KEITH AND SANDI CUNNINGHAM, AUTHORS OF *KEYS TO THE VAULT*

"My relationship with Tony has had a profound impact on my thinking as an executive. His executive coaching and counsel continues to have a positive effect on focusing my team and me on what matters. His principles and methodology provide a powerful tool set to increase employee engagement."
- PETER GALANIS, PRESIDENT, HEWLETT PACKARD, CANADA

"Tony, you have a truly outstanding Rolodex: you live up to your credo of action, execution, and connecting your network. You always exceed expectations! . . . Much needed content for business – this has the makings of a bestseller!" "
- ROMAN KIKTA, VENTURE CAPITALIST

"Tony helped me personally and my organization to clarify what's important and increase the tempo of my business."
- MITCHELL ALLEN, DEBT FOUNDATION ORGANIZATION, EO-DALLAS, TEXAS

"A person's life is richer when they find someone who lives their life on purpose and serves others with their unique gifts – thank you for enriching my life and continually pouring value into others!"
- ROSS LIGHTLE, CANADIAN BUSINESS COACH AND MENTOR

"Tony helped us get things done in hours, days, and weeks that might have taken months and years with less clarity and focus."
- DICK METZLER, EXECUTIVE, GREATWIDE LOGISTICS

"It doesn't matter where you start as every page has something you can take and use to improve your life or business."
- NORM FRIEND, CANADA'S LEADING FRANCHISE EXPERT

"By following the proven wisdom found in *Business Ground Rules* I am convinced that people will turn vision into reality faster and be much happier and more successful along the way."
– DAVID MATTSON, CEO, SANDLER SELLING SYSTEMS

Business Ground Rules
Be Great in Business

100 Lessons for Success

It's not just about getting rich.
It's about having a richer life.

TONY JEARY
THE RESULTS GUY™

PETER H. THOMAS
CHAIRMAN EMERITUS EO

With TAMMY KLING

Business Ground Rules: 100 Lessons for Success

© 2013 by Tony Jeary, Peter H. Thomas

Published by Carpenter's Son Publishing, Franklin, Tennessee

Cover Design by Debbie Manning Sheppard

Interior Layout Design by Suzanne Lawing

Edited by Andrew Toy

Printed in the United States of America

978-1-940262-22-2

Introduction

"The best way to predict the future is to create it."
- PETER DRUCKER

In order to be successful in life, you must start with focus and clarity. If you don't have clarity on your values, goals, and dreams, you can't get focused, and you won't get what you want.

This book will help you gain clarity on what it takes to be extraordinary—both in business and in your life. Inside you'll find the business principles that have transformed hundreds of high-achieving individuals, leaders, entrepreneurs, and companies we've worked with over the years.

Why are we writing this book?

Both of us have decades of experience in coaching others to success and operating successful businesses. Peter's *LifePilot* program has helped executives and CEOs across the world. Tony's strategic coaching with global CEOs has impacted millions, accelerating results. We've both observed that successful people share certain traits. Unsuccessful people do too. In fact, very few people have the kind of focus needed to become wealthy and make their goals a reality.

We hope the wisdom we share with you will transform your thinking and inspire you to take action. Both of us have studied, implemented, refined, lived out, advised, failed at, improved, and documented the distinctions we've included in this book.

It was the concept of goal setting that first brought us together, and it's the concept of goal setting—along with the rules for being your best in business—that brings us to you today. We met because we share a passion and commitment for designing our personal and professional lives, as well as how we choose to intentionally live our lives. Here's the story.

Tony's long-time coach and friend knew of someone who had more clarity and more documented goals than Tony. That was hard for Tony to believe because, at the time (in 2001), he had about fifty pages of documented goals covering what he wanted to become, share, and experience. Tony's friend gave him a copy of Peter's goals and that day was a catalyst in his life. Tony was inspired and began incorporating many of Peter's goals with his own because there was so much alignment. He eventually ended up with over one hundred pages of goals to live his life by.

Over the next twelve years, Tony and Peter met only once, at the home of mutual friends in North Dallas.

Three years after that meeting, Peter read Tony's monthly *Lessons from the Studio* on Measuring Everything, and sent an email to Tony. Just a few hours later, they had a lengthy phone conversation. Two weeks later, they boarded Peter's yacht in Canada for a private coaching session from Tony, and this book was born.

Have you ever had that kind of crossroads moment, where you know your world is about to expand? That day was powerful on several levels. First, we both decided to partner on a mentorship book that would change lives—one that would convince you that you can become wealthier if you want to. All you have to do is follow the rules we give you in this book and let us coach you to higher levels of success.

Second, it was so powerful that at seventy-five years young and with the remarkable success that Peter's had, he was still excited about coaching and has engaged Tony to be his "compression" coach for the rest of his life. After all, Peter has created many successful businesses and has coached thousands of millionaire entrepreneurs to success. Yet still he's willing to learn more!

Ask yourself if you're open to continual growth. Are you teachable? Are you committed to growth, even if it stretches you out of your comfort zone? We believe that your life's drive should be based on clear values. After all, how will you know if your values line up with what you want your results or outcome to be if you don't know what they are?

We are both interested in mentoring and impacting entrepreneurs and high achievers who really want to be their best. These individuals want to live extraordinary lives, and achieve strategically accelerating results. These successful people aren't just focused—they're extremely focused.

Extreme focus means having a dedication so strong that it requires letting go of what's distracting you from what you want. We've both had to let go of a lot of things in order to have what we want. And we both achieved the results we were working toward.

Think of it this way: More stuff, more friends, more activity, more businesses, more ideas, more meetings, and more events equal less "margin time." Less time to focus on what you really want means fewer true results. The opposite is equally true: Fewer distractions and more time devoted to your written goals equals more of the right results.

We developed a book that would be reader friendly, have a long shelf life for your library, provide great value, and be useful from many different angles. In doing so, we divided the core content into twelve categories:

1. Thinking
2. Clarity
3. Time
4. Strategic
5. Focus
6. Brand
7. Leadership
8. People
9. Money
10. Wealth
11. Execute
12. Health

This book can be read front to back or used as a reference guide by category, to be utilized based on your specific priorities. Above all, it offers user-friendly strategies for high achievers.

Mediocre advice is always available from the people in your life, from your Aunt Edna to your colleagues, to your friends on Facebook. But we both believe that it's important to take advice from someone who has done what you want to do, and has lived how you want to live.

We have both lived blessed lives. We've both authored many powerful books, mentored many top achievers, and given thousands of presentations. But most importantly, we have both won, lost, and then won again, both earning and losing millions. We aren't perfect, but we've learned a lot from our mistakes. Now we want to share our knowledge with you to sharpen you and make you even greater than you already are.

In the pages that follow, you will find one hundred lessons for your business, life, and growth, based on the distinctions, principles, and refinements we've both personally adopted. We want you to be richer financially, and in all areas of your life.

Enjoy learning the lessons/rules we've utilized in our own lives, and get ready to go to a higher level.

Let's get started!

Contents

I. THINKING

"Don't spend so much time trying to choose the perfect opportunity, that you miss the right opportunity."
– MICHAEL DELL

"The world as we have created it is a process of our thinking. It cannot be changed without changing our thinking."
- ALBERT EINSTEIN

"The mind is not a vessel to be filled, but a fire to be kindled."
- PLUTARCH

1.
Live Life on Purpose

Sure, good things can happen by accident. We've all found something delightful and forgotten in a coat pocket or under the sofa cushion. Finding extra money is good. Finding a lost key is good. But in our daily lives, is "good" really good enough?

High achievers don't settle for good; they seek awesome. And truly awesome things—hard-won and positive accomplishments—happen on purpose, as a result of thoughtful self-reflection, strong planning, and focused effort.

Measurement matters, and reflecting on the personal accomplishments in your life every once in a while (both past and present) can be motivating and inspiring. Measurement is an important step of living your life on purpose and developing your future. Both Peter and Tony have pages and pages of literally hundreds of goals they have both set and met throughout their lifetimes.

> **HIGH ACHIEVERS DON'T SETTLE FOR GOOD; THEY SEEK AWESOME.**

There is real power in documenting dreams and keeping an inventory of successes; life rarely happens the way you want it to by chance.

To start living your life on purpose, simply craft a list of valuable milestones you've already achieved. Whether you ran a marathon, earned a degree, met and married the partner of your dreams, established a company, or mastered juggling, begin making your list of the things you've already accomplished. Document realized educational goals, financial successes, personal accomplishments, and any other moments when your hard work has paid off.

Over time, it may become more formalized and find itself in chronological order as you meet new goals; but for now, simply take some time to look back on your undertakings, deeds, and successes. Going forward, you can organize it chronologically, by subject, or by importance. What's essential here is taking stock of how you've already lived a life of purpose, even if you weren't aware of it with this mindset. Reading through proof of your past achievements can be an important nudge when you feel stuck or uninspired. Likewise, browsing through documentation of where you've been and what you've done can be a powerful springboard for more purposeful success.

> COMMIT TO "MARGIN TIME" IN YOUR CALENDAR FOR THINKING, FLEXIBILITY, AND HEALTH-RELATED ACTIVITIES.
> –TONY JEARY

Now consider a few more questions: What do you want more of? Where would you rather be? Is there something of note you want to earn? How's the health of your bucket list? Asking yourself these kinds of introspective questions—and writing down the answers—will allow you to make smart changes and strategic decisions that will purposely propel you forward toward what you most want to accomplish, whatever the scope or size.

Don't become sidetracked with trying to create a perfect and complete list before starting; the best way to get to work is simply to get to work! Focus on a goal you've documented. You can choose the easiest one, or maybe the most enticing—whatever best suits your motivation. Write down what needs to happen in order for that goal to be a success. Identify anyone who can, will, or should help you. And be sure to give yourself a deadline so that you create a little positive anxiety about reaching your goal. Now, get going. It really is as simple as that.

Solid accomplishments are so much better than happy accidents, and that's a distinction that truly successful people know and live—on purpose.

2.
Have Fun. Make Money.

Business is a serious thing. It requires a lot of thought, and sometimes lives hang in the balance because you're winning or you're losing. But don't forget that business is life; and in life, you have to have fun. If you're not having fun, what's the point?

This is an important rule for the eager entrepreneur to understand. Throughout the stressful moments, you have to view having fun as a motivator and a priority.

> SURROUND YOURSELF WITH THE RIGHT PEOPLE—THOSE ARE THE PEOPLE YOU'RE GOING TO HAVE FUN WITH.

Love your life! Beyond that, do business and surround yourself professionally with people you love and who energize you. Being energized can be a tremendous asset that greatly alters your chances of success. Surround yourself with the right people—those are the people you're going to have fun with. Make sure these people are going to fit your team, your culture, and your idea of what you want your business to be. Do they gel with your personality? If they don't, it won't work well.

> IT'S NOT JUST ABOUT MAKING MONEY; IT'S ABOUT DEVELOPING A LIFE WHERE EVERY DAY IS A WEEKEND.
> –TONY JEARY

How do you want your life to look? Do you want to be sitting in a retirement home when you're eighty doing crossword puzzles? We don't. We want to do deals, help people grow, have fun, and make money. How many times have you heard someone groan about their job? Don't let that be you.

The old saying "you only live once" is an obvious and simple truth. Doesn't it make sense to maximize the experience?

3.
Eliminate Blind Spots from Your Belief Window

Your Belief Window is how you perceive and understand everything in your life—the way you see the world, your role in that world, and the relationships you have with others. It includes everything you believe to be true, false, correct, incorrect, appropriate, inappropriate, possible, and impossible. It frames all your views of people, places, and things, and creates the perceptions and feelings you have about everything. It also influences the actions you take regarding those same people, places, and things. This window allows information you consider important to enter your mind and be retained, and blocks out the things that you do not consider important. It screens information and circumstances you don't think you need.

> WE ALL HAVE BLIND SPOTS THAT OBSCURE WHAT WE COULD AND SHOULD SEE PAST, AND THESE CAN REALLY HINDER RESULTS.

But sometimes principles that cross our Belief Window can be wrong, outdated, or even just limiting. We all have Blind Spots that obscure what we could and should see past, and these can really hinder results. But how are we to know what our Blind Spots are, to expand our frame of reference? I believe there are four core ways to do this:

1) Engage a mentor to pour into you
2) Hire a coach to sharpen your thinking
3) Reach out to trusted colleagues

> OUR *BELIEF WINDOW* CONTAINS THE PRINCIPLES WE BELIEVE TO BE TRUE. CONSTANTLY CHECK FOR BLIND SPOTS, DISTINCTIONS, AND PERSPECTIVES TO ENSURE YOUR PRINCIPLES ARE ACCURATE AND UP TO DATE.
> —TONY JEARY

4) Feed your mind purposefully through books, videos, and audios

High achievers realize that they need and want to know more about topics relevant to their success, and they keep themselves relevant and updated through conscious effort. This conscious learning and investigation will help expand your Belief Window, which, in turn, will help you make smarter decisions.

Take a good look at your Belief Window and do some refinement. Get the opinion or perspective of a trusted coach, and intentionally expand your knowledge base on things important to you. Once you clean off those old, incorrect principles on your window, you'll see so much farther and your success will exponentially increase.

4.
Select Mentors Carefully and Understand What "Mentor" Means

Yes, you need a mentor—preferably more than one. If you do not have any, it's time to get some. You can only be as successful as your own mind allows you to be, if you act alone. Entrepreneurs are often used to going it alone; but if you want to be more successful than you currently are, you'll have to rely on others to get you there. Mentors can be a phenomenal resource because the right ones have traveled the journey that you are embarking on. There's always someone with more wisdom and knowledge than you to learn from.

Remember that the most successful entrepreneurs are willing to learn. They never assume they know it all or have all the answers. If you want to grow and advance faster, be intentional about your mentors and coaches. Don't just work with mentors you know and like; find someone who's doing what you want to do, even if you don't know them.

Who are your mentors in business or in life in general? A mentor isn't necessarily a family member or a friend. This person is not necessarily a coach either, because a mentor offers his or her wisdom for free. This person is someone who is willing to give you advice about how to run your business, attract more clients, or implement certain valuable processes. Every mentoring session should include discussion that uncovers options, solutions, and new ideas.

Mentors give back. They want to give back to the world and they want to give advice because it is part of their legacy and contribution. We recommend having at least five mentors, since both of us have personally benefited immensely from mentor-mentee relationships. Even though Tony is a world-renowned business strategist, has owned dozens of businesses, and has advised over 1,000 clients; and even though Peter is seventy-five, wealthy, and has done hundreds of deals—we both know that we don't know everything! That's what mentors are for.

I (Tony) wanted to raise exceptional kids, so I found mentors who had already achieved that. I even found mentors who had two girls, just like I do. I carefully chose those mentors who had successful daughters and asked them to share their knowledge and time with my family and me. It really is valuable to get the opinion and insight of another person who is equally committed to your success.

> THERE'S ALWAYS SOMEONE WITH MORE WISDOM AND KNOWLEDGE THAN YOU TO LEARN FROM.

When I (Peter) started my first company, my lawyer told me that I needed to appoint some directors who could give the company wisdom, direction, and strategy. I was only twenty-eight years old and had not met enough people then who I felt could give me the advice that I needed, so I got creative. At home, we had a book of black-and-white photographs of John F. Kennedy, Martin Luther King, Ghandi, and Ernest Hemingway, among other famous people. I knew they had a lot of wisdom and could advise me with what I needed to do, so I cut their pictures out and framed them. As challenges came into my life, I would ask each one of them what they would do about the particular issue. I found that JFK was the business advisor. MLK was the person who could tell me what was right and what was wrong; he was a wonderful decision maker. Ghandi was my spiritual guide, and Mr. Hemingway was the writer and rogue advisor. If I wanted an excuse to have a little fun, I would be sure to ask Ernest.

The purpose of this kind of "virtual mentorship" is to open your mind to the idea that you do not need living mentors (although they are great and you should have them), but you can have access to the wisdom of the ages if you use your imagination. Once you select who your virtual mentors are going to be, immediately go down to your favorite bookstore, buy an autobiography of your first mentor, and read it cover to cover. No matter who your virtual mentor is, you can read or download something on him or her and learn.

Leverage your mentors and get as much wisdom as you can from them. By listening to and observing the habits of those more successful than yourself in selected areas and then modeling that behavior, you will constantly elevate your levels of thought and success.

5.
Look Deep . . . "There's a Pony in There Somewhere!"

Everyone who knows me (Peter) knows my philosophy: There's a pony in there somewhere! This comes from an old story about a little boy who wanted a pony for Christmas. On Christmas morning, he woke up to find his Christmas tree surrounded not by gifts, but by a gigantic pile of manure. While all his friends stood around feeling sorry for him, knowing he didn't get what he wanted most, the little boy began wildly and happily digging through the pile of manure. "I just know there's a pony in there somewhere," he exclaimed.

That's how I've been all my life. My colleague, Charlie, watched me sort through and reject over 500 deals last summer when I started my newest venture, Thomas Franchise Solutions; and indeed, there was one pony in there: Dogtopia. It became our first deal.

> I WANT TO SUCCEED, AND I WANT TO FIND THE PERFECT PROJECT. BUT IT HAS TO BE THE RIGHT PROJECT.
> - PETER THOMAS

In the early seventies, I "found" Century 21 Canada among all the possible deals I could have done.

In the eighties, I "found" literally hundreds of real estate projects and created Samoth Capital Corp. I put in all the properties I had created and took that organization public and raised hundreds of millions.

In the nineties, I "found" Westover Hills, one of the largest tracts of land in San Antonio, Texas, paying $9,000,000 and returning the partners over $120,000,000.

In 2000, I "found" the land to create The Four Seasons Hotel, in Scottsdale, Arizona.

In 2012, I "found" Dogtopia and created Thomas Franchise Solutions.

I was not born wealthy; these opportunities just kept presenting themselves after a lot of digging. As the projects came, along came the wisdom to figure out how to do them, how to find the money, and how to find the partners.

My attitude says there are ponies everywhere if you are willing to shovel the manure aside. Sometimes it seems like a lot of manure, but just keep shoveling with the faith that there is a pony in there somewhere.

I am motivated by the thrill of the search. I want to succeed, and I want to find the perfect project. But it has to be the right project. I don't want to come up with a duck when I'm looking for that pony.

So when people call me or any of my successful entrepreneurial pals "lucky," it's a special kind of luck: the luck of a person willing to work hard enough to get to the bottom of the pile and see what might be there, all the while believing in that pony.

6.
Do What Wealthy People Do (Think How Wealthy People Think)

We are not advocating for only material wealth. But it's good to have money because money can offer you freedom. Money is a blessing; and if you're an entrepreneur, you need it to fuel your dreams. If financial freedom and growing monetary wealth are your goals, that's great too. We prefer to live wealthy in all areas of life. Tony calls it "Living in the Black."

In order to get money and create wealth (however you define it), you need to think how wealthy people think. If you keep running into brick walls and you're not sure why, find someone who is truly wealthy and emulate their philosophies. You could tap a business owner you've admired from afar, or it might be a family friend or an elder. Interview this individual about their thought patterns, life and business outlooks, and personal style. Then model that person and live the way they live.

> WEALTHY, SUCCESSFUL PEOPLE HAVE SPECIFIC, DAILY HABITS, AND SO DO POOR, UNSUCCESSFUL PEOPLE.

When you start practicing this on a regular basis, you might find that there are a lot of differences between how that person is living and how you live. We have found that when comparing wealthy people to people who are not wealthy, there are extreme differences, specifically in their habits.

31

Wealthy, successful people have specific, daily habits, and so do poor, unsuccessful people. Please note that we are not stating that poor people are unsuccessful. You won't find that theory anywhere in this book. What we are saying is that poor people have similar habits, and rich people have similar habits (and some of their habits can be found in books like *The 7 Habits of Highly Successful People* or *The One Minute Manager*). Publishers don't publish books about the habits of poor or unsuccessful people. Yet, they do share certain traits, such as a lack of focus, a scarcity mentality, and a pattern of repeatedly not succeeding.

So what are the habits of highly successful people? We believe that most successful people:

- Have a routine: They rise early, start the day with purpose, nourish themselves regularly, and have other predictable behaviors.
- Are disciplined: They meet deadlines, deliver on promises, and keep their word.
- Concentrate on overall well-being: They care for their bodies, minds, and businesses, and treat them like the irreplaceable tools they are.
- Have focus: They figure out what needs to be done and stay on track through the activities that matter most.
- Continually learn: They read, engage mentors or advanced education, then find ways to incorporate what they've learned into their life.
- Stay positive: They look on the bright side, are solution-oriented, and seek success instead of dwelling on misery.

What are some habits you can refine or adopt that mirror those of successful, wealthy people you admire most?

7.
Avoid Negative Thoughts

As we wrote in Rule #6, we have seen that successful people have similar habits. The same can be said of unsuccessful people and their thoughts. Often while the successful leader is thinking about how something can be done, the unsuccessful individual is thinking of why it *can't* be done.

Garbage can fill your home just as easily as beautiful furniture. Obviously, beautiful furniture is more valuable than the garbage we remove from our homes when it starts to smell or when the container is full.

A negative thought is like a piece of garbage. Negative thoughts clutter our mind and use the same mental real estate that positive ones do, even though they do not have the same importance or power. You wouldn't keep garbage in your living spaces, so why would you keep a negative thought in your brain? You need to eliminate your negative thoughts in the same way you would take the garbage out when it starts to stink or occupies too much space.

> HAVE A SOLUTION-ORIENTED ATTITUDE AND A "HOW DO WE?" VERSUS A "WHY WE CAN'T?" MINDSET.
> –TONY JEARY

8.
Value Your Daily Solitude

You're probably energized and full of ideas often, right? High achievers are doers and creators. We like to create new things, and that energy often leads to a domino effect where we create, inspire, and motivate the lives around us and continually draw people into our world. But then the inevitable occurs as that world becomes louder and more cluttered. How do you get off of the treadmill of responding to emails, getting sucked into meaningless meetings or activities, and remain focused? You have to make time.

Don't underestimate the importance of solitude. Having time alone to dream or just think is important. Don't expect this time to always happen naturally—you have to make time for solitude. Life is fast! Go enjoy the beauty of nature; put on some music, close your eyes, and relax.

Solitude is so important for your soul. It can refresh

> PEOPLE WHO DON'T MAKE A POINT TO SPEND TIME ALONE FIND THEMSELVES CLUTTERED WITH THE IDEAS AND PLANS OF OTHERS.
> -PETER THOMAS

your mind and help clear out any cobwebs. It doesn't matter if you take the moment alone first thing in the morning, or during the middle of the day, as long as you create that space.

People who don't make a point to spend time alone find themselves cluttered with the ideas and plans of others. Your body and mind are your most important assets; and if you don't take time alone, how can you be as productive and fresh as you need to be? Maintain your body and your mind by being intentional about solitude.

Some people take a personal sabbatical or retreat—two or three days alone in a hotel, on a boat, or on a beach—to simply relax, refresh, and regenerate their mind. They take time to pray, meditate, contemplate, get a massage, journal thoughts, and relax. Others spend one night a year in a hotel room alone—not in a hotel for business, but in a hotel specifically with the idea of having twenty-four hours of solitude. They turn off the TV and phone to be alone with their thoughts. Or, if that's not for you, take a few hours one day and go for a walk outdoors, or in a park.

As wonderful as solitude is (and as refreshing as it is), it can require some sacrifices because it means spending time away from people, places, and things you love, including your family or business. You will often gain a clear mind, stimulate new ideas, and most of the time gain a renewed sense of purpose. We say that makes the trade-off well worth it!

Streamlining and simplifying life is a must for high achievers. Solitude will help you think better, lead better, and see what's ahead more clearly.

9.
Get a Coach

Coaching isn't just for professional athletes. The concept of coaching has been in place for decades. Top CEOs have coaches who guide them with personal and professional advice. Entrepreneurs have coaches who challenge and inspire them to be their best. Do you have a powerful coach?

It's worth noting that a coach is different than a mentor: Coaches are paid; mentors are not. Coaches offer paid advice, while a mentor is generally free advice from someone who wants to give back. A colleague can be a trusted advisor who coaches you, but don't confuse them with a coach. Some people say, "I have a trusted colleague, so I don't need a coach." If this is your thinking, you may want to reframe it. Coaching is an investment in yourself, your business, and your results.

> COACHING IS AN INVESTMENT IN YOURSELF, YOUR BUSINESS, AND YOUR RESULTS.

Everyone should have one (or more) mentor. And everyone should have a coach. I (Tony) was sitting in my *Strategic Acceleration* Studio a few years back strategizing with the CIO of Deloitte, and I was saying that as of that time, I'd had the same coach for more than twenty-five years. This man was shocked. He said, "You've had the same man for twenty-five years helping you succeed in business and helping you win in life? That's longer than you've been married." I said yes. He said, "Do you know how fortunate you are to have someone in your life that long supports you in being successful?" I had not thought about it in those terms before and appreciated his pointing this out. I needed to show more gratitude for my long-term friend and coach, Mark Pantak. This man serves up the best books, introduces me to special people, makes me aware of Blind Spots, councils me on my thinking, and sharpens my vision. He prays for my wisdom and success often. I sent him an iPad the very next day with a special note of thanks.

Successful people reach higher levels through coaches who impact their thinking. Coaches can help you reach your peak performance and operate often at higher levels—like the mastery level.

Choose someone who matches your values. Find an expert who already has success in your field and has proven success in the direction you want to go. Find someone who has done what you want to do, who studies, has an arsenal, has real experience, and of course has a sincere desire to help you win.

10.
Deploy the AMC™ Test in Your Business

AMC™ stands for Attitude, Motivation, and Commitment. Before we hire people, we test them to assess how they would complement our culture and align with our standards. Are they cheerful? Is the glass half full or half empty? Are they results-driven and upbeat? Are they going to add positivity?

It's not necessarily skills or resumes that will determine how well people will perform. The strength of an individual or team often lies in their attitude, motivation, and commitment.

> THE STRENGTH OF AN INDIVIDUAL OR TEAM OFTEN LIES IN THEIR ATTITUDE, MOTIVATION, AND COMMITMENT.
> - PETER THOMAS

If you're not sure which candidate you want to bring into your business, the AMC™ mental check is a good way to identify what people you want in your world, helping you succeed. To confirm one's AMC™, you can use a handmade pen-and-paper questionnaire or computer-based survey of some kind (we use and recommend the DISC assessment; see www.personalityinsights.com). If you create a questionnaire, we suggest you augment it by a series of interview questions tailored to your organization's specific needs. However you decide to assess candidates, you will want to uncover information about how they can be expected to:

• Operate emotionally under stress as well as during calmer times

(Behavioral/situational "What would you do if . . . " questions are great here)

- Respond to a negative customer or negative personal interaction
- Represent your brand and philosophies
- Pursue success, approach teamwork, and work to your standards
- Stick with your team based on previous work history queries
- Respect authority and support overall morale
- Be accountable, reliable, empowered, and self-sufficient
- Deploy personal values and ethics that match your own
- Use the strengths of their personality style, and overcome weaknesses/challenges

A recent study discovered that 46 percent of new hires failed within 18 months, and that 89 percent of the time it was due to attitude, not a lack of technical skills. Make sure you work with people who really add to your organization—not cause upheaval. Use the AMC™ test when it comes to hiring and partnering with people to ensure you create the best (life) team possible.

11.
Ask Your Coaches and Mentors for Their Recommended Reading Lists

The smartest people we've met, advise, and work with love to learn—they thrive on new ideas and read a lot of books, study videos, and pore over articles that help change and challenge their thinking. Talk to any high achiever and chances are they'll mention a book that influenced their life at some point and helped them achieve their dreams. (See our list of favorite books in the back.)

The same is true for us. Each year, we read, study, and recap dozens of books, not only for our own learning, but to help mentor and coach others. I (Tony) recognized two decades ago that when I would read a book, I often would only retain a very small portion of the author's content, even after investing hours of highlighting. Now for over 20 years, I have been recapping my books. That's right. I read and study between 50 and 100 books a year. I highlight them and type them into recaps that I can go back and study over and over. I have thousands of recaps now that I provide to my special clients to help them advance their thinking and learning.

Ask your mentors and coaches which books and videos they've studied that helped them get where they are. Nearly every successful person we know will mention reading the book *Think and Grow Rich*. It's not a coincidence, either.

High achievers get real results and avoid stagnation by seeking constant information and by valuing self-improvement. New information can be gathered through reading trade and industry magazines, newspapers, books, and other publications, including brief recaps or abstracts that save time by condensing information.

You can't attend every seminar, self help session, or motivational meeting. But you can quickly download a book on your tablet or mobile device that will create new ideas, catalyze change, and help you get where you're going in life.

THE SMARTEST PEOPLE LOVE TO LEARN.

A good coach will always have a new book, article, or video to share with you; so ask them what they're studying and be prepared to take notes.

12.
Foster Joy, Entertainment, and Inspiration

Create "wow" moments that inspire and engage your people. Make joy, entertainment, and inspiration a part of both your business and personal life, and weave in great experiences. Ask yourself, "Do I continually look for ways to bring motivation to my people?" If the answer is no, you can improve upon this area immediately.

People often go through life content with average experiences and the status quo. Living your best life means looking out for those exceptional moments that change you. And by change you, I don't mean major change, although that does happen sometimes. I mean those things that change your thinking, challenge you to do more, and inspire you to be a better you. Look at yourself and ask, for example, "Are my meetings boring?" So many meetings are. Perhaps you should bring videos and guest speakers, and foster laughter and appropriate business entertainment in your meetings more often. Think about it. Do you like to go to boring meetings?

> LIVING YOUR BEST LIFE MEANS LOOKING OUT FOR THOSE EXCEPTIONAL MOMENTS THAT CHANGE YOU.

When I (Tony) see that someone is bored or uncomfortable, I immediately want to meet that need and help make a shift. Provide inspiration for your clients, too. Meetings don't have to be the only place you change. Make your calls more impactful by standing up and walking around more often, pouring energy into the phone. Wake up each day with the commitment that whomever you meet, you will bring joy and inspiration, putting smiles on people's faces. Life can be focused and yet inspiring. Go to another level.

13.
Sharpen Your Sword with Precise Communication

How many emailed articles a week do you trash or ignore? How many books would you like to read but just don't have the time? How many newspapers are left unread, beyond the headlines? This glut of words has become a factor in the way you compete for business and communicate your value. Information is coming at us at lightning speed.

> IF THE RESULTS YOU'VE BEEN GETTING HAVE NOT BEEN WHAT YOU EXPECT AND WANT, YOU NEED TO BECOME WILLING TO CHANGE THE WAY YOU THINK SO YOU CAN CHANGE YOUR RESULTS.
>
> –TONY JEARY

While the digital age makes it easier to compile and share text, the competition for the time people invest in reading has been increased dramatically. When you're communicating with others, you need to be concise, so sharpen your sword! If you can't get your message down to one page, you will probably not be heard. As a leader, teach others to do the same.

Most people use far more words to make their point than is really necessary. Their writing rambles on and on, talking about things that aren't essential. That works for a novel, but not in business communications. If you want to communicate or sell an idea, you have to frame the important things and capture the value proposition in as few words as possible.

This seems obvious. So why do people have such a hard time achieving it? It's because people often lack clarity regarding what they most need to communicate.

And the key to achieving clarity here is found in the word "why." It relates to the positive perceptions people have about purpose and value. When it comes to communicating your ideas through conversation, email, or phone calls, simply ask yourself, "What's the objective or actions I'd like to get accomplished?" This will give clarity and is the key ingredient that will make your messages powerful.

> IF YOU CAN'T GET YOUR MESSAGE DOWN TO ONE PAGE, YOU WILL PROBABLY NOT BE HEARD.

14.
Help Others Win

From day one, we encounter competition—on the playground, in the classroom, on the playing field. Later we compete with others for grades, educational benefits, careers, and achievements. It seems we are wired to compete (at some level), and that often leads to a mindset of "one-upping," outshining, and outperforming others. But truly smart high achievers help others win, which directly impacts the speed of results they experience. This is a principle both Peter and Tony live out today.

When Tony was a kid, his dad taught him the most important business principle of his life: "Give value: Do more than is expected!" It is the foundation of his success, and in fact, his entire business centers around helping their clients win often by giving value and doing more than what is expected.

> **SUCCESSFUL PEOPLE HELP OTHERS BECOME SUCCESSFUL TOO.**

Peter also loves to over-deliver and add value to another's life and growth. And when we first decided to write this book, we knew we both shared this philosophy. It is the foundation of the success we both enjoy.

Bottom line: Successful people help others become successful too. This rule is powerful because it requires a paradigm shift for many. Those who cannot make the paradigm shift from a "scarcity, win at all costs" mentality to a "winning by helping others win" mindset will not operate in mastery. In order to be the best, have the best, and deliver the best results, you must be completely comfortable and confident that you will win when you help others win—it's a must.

How many times have you encountered a colleague or service pro-

45

vider who seemed to enjoy saying no? They want to give as little as possible, and they feel good doing it. We've all seen this principle of scarcity in action at the airline ticket counter. Just try asking for a free upgrade or any consideration and see what the response is. Many agents want to say no before you even finish your sentence. Certainly there are guidelines an agent has to live by, and yet isn't it so refreshing to work with an agent of any kind where you know they want to help you win and they think, talk, and do more than you might expect to help you?

Another thought…We've all heard the term "buyer's remorse." It is a polite term for the way people feel when they have purchased something or decided on something and the item or the experience perhaps did not meet their felt needs and expectations. The negatives of disappointment are significant, but there is a huge positive impact on results when products or services exceed expectations.

When we buy something that exceeds our expectations, we are often blown away by our good fortune. We can't believe that we "got all of this" for what we paid. What we got could be a combination of product, quality, customer support, the effect the product had on our lives, or any other thing that makes us happy about the money we spent. When our expectations are exceeded, we become walking advertisements and testimonials for the product or service. Every time we run across a friend with a similar need, we tell them about what we got for what we paid. We are what Ken Blanchard calls "raving fans" at that point, and a raving fan can't be tempted and lured away by competitors. This is the kind of customer that leads to growth and great results for any business.

When you help someone win, you often create a fan for life. Embed this rule into your organization.

15.
Express Gratitude

Are you happy about what you've achieved? What are you grateful for? Being grateful enables you to remember how fortunate and blessed you are, and gratitude impacts the way you view life.

Successful leaders regularly express gratitude for the positive things in their lives. Some even keep gratitude journals or lists. Gratitude is an important trait to possess, because when people realize you're grateful, they often want to keep giving. This doesn't just extend to your personal life; it obviously extends to business as well.

> **SUCCESSFUL LEADERS REGULARLY EXPRESS GRATITUDE FOR THE POSITIVE THINGS IN THEIR LIVES.**

Authentic gratitude in business will go a long way. Gratitude means that you truly care about others and you recognize their gifts and talents. If you have employees, this is extremely important to cultivate. If you have colleagues and customers, think of ways that you can let them know how important they are to you. Even if you have managers, bosses, or a CEO above you, it's important to manage up, down, and sideways and one great way is to be authentic and show your gratitude. Not sure how? It's quite simple. Just see the positive in everyone you meet and celebrate it.

In addition to reviewing achievements, it is important to remember the people who make a difference in our lives and to show appreciation. Take a look back at the previous year and the people who touched your life along the way. Now take some time to list those individuals and ask yourself if they know how much you appreciate them. If they don't, what are you waiting for?

Aesop said, "Gratitude is the sign of noble souls." It is noble, indeed, to be thankful as such a gesture shows humility and selflessness. When we step outside our sometimes-egocentric world to recognize that we cannot and do not control everything, we can acknowledge our day-to-day existence as a gift. Being grateful for whatever benefits we receive enables us to remember how fortunate and blessed we really are. This habit of expressing gratitude is also a fast track to a more positive outlook.

> PRACTICE AUTHENTICITY—BE REAL, BE YOURSELF. MAKE OTHER PEOPLE FEEL GOOD.
> –PETER THOMAS

16.
Beware of King Arthur's Disease

Initial and early triumph is inspiring and encouraging, exciting and contagious. It's like a drug. But, there's danger if you don't balance the excitement with the strategy and skill that owning your own business requires. This feeling of invincibility can cloud judgment and result in poor decision-making based on ignored risks.

Peter gave this malady—the feeling of being invincible—a name, hoping that others could also recognize the symptoms before they turned into the full-blown illness. He calls this malady "King Arthur's Disease," and it does not discriminate.

At first, the victim feels as invincible as King Arthur; nothing can destroy him. He feels he can continue to go into battle (or business) just like King Arthur and come out victorious. He's drunk on the adrenaline of success.

Ambitious individuals can get so caught up in the thrill of the chase that they overlook risks. They make another acquisition or deal, becoming so overconfident that they begin to believe that every deal will result in success. If they have four or five successes, they start to believe they're the smartest person in the room. They stop seeking advice from others. And that's when the sobering moment happens.

We have both had experiences where we lost it all, and it taught us valuable lessons: Don't operate in a vacuum, and don't let success go

> AMBITIOUS INDIVIDUALS CAN GET SO CAUGHT UP IN THE THRILL OF THE CHASE THAT THEY OVERLOOK RISKS.
> - PETER THOMAS

to your head. Get the best professional advisors you can obtain. Build a Life Team around you (see #71). Don't rely solely on your own judgment, because advisors can give you feedback you may not have thought of and insight you may not have seen. It's okay if you have vision they don't have; reach out to mentors and other Life Team members who know your values and priorities. And learn to spot the symptoms of "King Arthur's Disease," which can be a financially fatal illness.

We all know what happened to Camelot in the end—it collapsed. This disease is as dangerous to your career as it was to King Arthur, who rushed into battle without armor, against a foe he knew nothing about, because he had not done his research. Fortunately, we overcame King Arthur's Disease by checking in with our values and putting life back into perspective. We haven't felt the symptoms again since.

17.
Avoid FUD

There are three factors that inhibit most humans from reaching their goals and achieving their potential: Fear, Uncertainty, and Doubt (FUD). When we give into FUD, we set ourselves up for failure. I (Peter) share a story in my *LifePilot* seminar that illustrates the way FUD can work, and how you can overcome it:

> FUD is fear, uncertainty, and doubt. When I was thirty-five, I started buying the rights to Century 21 in Canada. I was excited and began to share my goal to do that with a business partner. The partner said it would never work, and when I asked him to invest money, he said no. So I went to another guy. He said it was a stupid idea. I asked my lawyer; he said no. Even my wife didn't think it was a good idea! The feedback I got ranged from, "It'll never work," to "No realtor is going to wear that gold jacket to work." Century 21 had an interesting brand in which you could identify the realtors by their gold jackets.
>
> So at that time, I really bought into the vision and no one else around me did. I had a vision that no one else could see. I forged ahead despite the warnings and naysayers because I believed in it! And it was a success. Later, I sold it for many millions. Sometimes everyone else is blind and your vision is crystal clear.

NEVER ALLOW YOURSELF TO GIVE A MEDIOCRE PERFORMANCE, NO MATTER WHAT THE CIRCUMSTANCES.

In my early selling days, I always had a 4x6 card taped hanging from the rear-view window of my car. On the card was written in capital letters: "THIS WILL BE THE BEST PRESENTATION I HAVE EVER GIVEN." It was my reminder that I would not experience any fear, uncertainty, or doubt. Sure enough, every time I put on a presentation, I made it the best presentation I had ever given.

> THE BELIEF THAT GREATNESS ALREADY EXISTS BECOMES THE ENEMY OF MASTERY.
> –TONY JEARY

It is so important to always give your best. Never allow yourself to give a mediocre performance, no matter what the circumstances, even if fear creeps in. Sometimes your best performances can come when it is most difficult for you to perform.

So what if you start to feel a case of the FUD coming on? The way to overcome it is to maintain clarity, stay focused on your goal, be persistent, and execute. Don't allow fear or uncertainty or doubt to rule your emotions, thoughts, or actions. If you really believe in something, keep doing it until you achieve your goal with a perfect performance.

18.
Give Back

People generally live their life in three stages: the learning years, the earning years, and the returning years. When you're young and fresh out of school or in your early twenties, it's all about learning. Next, in building an adult life, it becomes mostly about earning, building a career and business ventures, establishing a family, and building wealth.

The third stage is the returning years. This stage can (and should) happen simultaneously with other stages as much as possible, but we have found where there is much given, there is much expected. Make an intentional effort to give back to those less fortunate than yourself, or even to those less knowledgeable than yourself.

> **FIND SOMETHING YOU CAN BE PASSIONATE ABOUT AND GIVE BACK, EITHER PERSONALLY OR FINANCIALLY.**

Giving back can come in the form of time or money. After the tragic loss of my son in 2000, I (Peter) focused on social entrepreneurship and wanted to share my experience and philosophy of values-based living and leadership with others. I founded LifePilot, which seeks to empower people to live fulfilling, balanced lives and to realize their highest personal potential.

Both of us have established Youth Advisory Boards to mentor the young minds that are our future, and to encourage their ideas for innovations and initiatives.

Find something you can be passionate about and give back, either personally or financially. It will come back to you in more ways than you expect.

19.
Lead a No-Excuses Culture

This simply means that each person takes responsibility for whatever the situation is. Whether you did it or didn't do it, own up to it and say, "Hey, let's get it done," with the emphasis on getting results, versus pointing fingers.

In our research of organizations, we found that the higher the person's self-esteem, the more they will accept the responsibility and want to take action to get the desired result. This shows that fostering a positive mentality, appreciation, and true ownership within your organization can matter a lot. Help all your people grow and see themselves in the best light possible, while being genuine.

> MAKE IT KNOWN THAT YOU'RE NOT AFTER EXCUSES; YOU'RE AFTER RESULTS.

Make it known (with written Performance Standards) that you're not after excuses; you're after results. An example of this no-excuses culture could be that if you're going to have a discussion and bring up a road-block or an issue, you're also required to offer a solution simultaneously. This is a great kind of system to have in place to help people move away from a defensive response, and instead move toward getting the desired result.

II. CLARITY

*"The first step toward creating an improved future
is developing the ability to envision it.
Vision will ignite the fire of passion that fuels our commitment to
do whatever it takes to achieve excellence. Only vision allows us
to transform dreams of greatness into the reality of achievement
through human action. Vision has no boundaries
and knows no limits.
Our vision is what we become in life."*
- TONY DUNGY

*"Chase the vision, not the money,
and the money will end up following you."*
- TONY HSIEH

*"Gratitude unlocks the fullness of life.
It turns what we have into enough, and more.
It turns denial into acceptance, chaos to order, confusion to clarity.
It can turn a meal into a feast,
a house into a home, a stranger into a friend.
Gratitude makes sense of our past, brings peace for today,
and creates a vision for tomorrow."*
– MELODY BEATTIE

20.
Clarity: Get It and Use It

What do you want out of life? Your business? Your deals? Clarity, focus, and successful execution are essential pillars of entrepreneurism, and necessary tools for getting what you want. The most successful people design their own lives, and then live their lives on purpose. But the first step is clarity.

The definition of clarity is: Understanding and documenting your targets clearly and determining the "why" behind reaching them (personally and professionally). It's about developing a clear vision, outlining priorities and objectives, and tackling goals with a real sense of urgency and focus. Clarity is achieved when ideas and concepts are clearly explained and presented internally and externally; it's when we know where we are in relation to where we want to go.

When clarity is lost, or never achieved in the first place, it is almost impossible to generate the kind of focus necessary to establish a dynamic organization capable of acting swiftly and deftly on a daily basis. What you're left with instead is a struggling, underperforming organization and frustrated employees eager to jump ship.

The requirements for clarity are specific with respect to three issues:

1. Purpose—relates to the "why" of things, thought through and documented
2. Value—relates to the real benefits that can be acquired (for all stakeholders to win)
3. Objectives—relates to the premise that unless objectives are stated clearly and understood by all, the likelihood of achieving them is slim

You have to ask yourself the hard questions: "Why do I want to buy a franchise? Why do I want to be in the business I'm in?" Are you building a business to sell or are you building a family business you want to pass down? Be clear on what you want and utilize tools along the way. (Visit www.strategicacceleration.com for a free assessment and many free tools.)

When you have an authentic vision, things happen. If you have no vision, there is nothing to tie your objectives to and nothing to measure your progress or performance against. When you have clarity about your vision, you discover yourself being pulled toward it and all you have to do is follow the connecting opportunities that carry you along, allowing you to make connections faster.

THE MOST SUCCESSFUL PEOPLE DESIGN THEIR OWN LIVES, AND THEN LIVE THEIR LIVES ON PURPOSE.

Think about a time when you've been excited and regenerated at the thought of achieving a big goal. For an entrepreneur, there's nothing like the adrenaline rush of having complete clarity about what it is you want to achieve. When you have clarity, you get that excitement that builds and fuels your energy toward that dream. The results you achieve will often come faster than you may have thought possible.

Clarity and focus together form the basis of execution. So get completely clear about the things that you want and then take action.

21.
Align Goals with Your Values

Is your inner world in line with your outer world? People often set goals for what they want in life but their daily and weekly activities don't reflect their goals and values. Think of someone who says they value family first, yet they work so much that they don't have time to spend with their family. They miss baseball games, are a no-show at the dance recitals, and they're never home for dinner because they're constantly at the office. The stress continuously builds because there's a gap between what they want and what they do.

LEARN HOW TO FOCUS ON YOUR VALUES NOW, SO YOU CAN LIVE BY THEM IN ALL SEASONS AND AVOID THE PITFALLS IN LIFE.

We've all been there. I (Peter) got into some major financial difficulties halfway through my career, and for several years I feared I would lose everything I had earned. When I was in the deepest part of the situation, I had a very good talk with myself and evaluated where I was. I picked up a pencil and a pad of paper and put down my assets. They were good health, freedom, family, friendships, reputation, relationships, self-esteem, wisdom, good work ethic, success, integrity, being a mentor, being a leader, lots of love, and the assets went on and on. In fact the only thing that I could not put on the list was money.

I had been feeling sorry for myself before I made the list, but when I saw all the assets that I did have in writing, I felt like a very lucky man. I realized that if I had to give away one of my assets, it would have been money because I could always get that back, but I could not get some of the other assets back if I lost them. I quit feeling sorry for myself and started living like I was grateful for what I did have. During the time of my financial recovery, I ran the NY marathon, learned how to fly a helicopter, wrote a book, and used the excess time to rebuild my business, in addition to traveling all over the world with my family.

Once you list all your values, you will realize just how "wealthy" you are too, and that money is only one of your many assets—and not the most important one by far. In all likelihood it is the first thing you would give away if your values were threatened.

Get clarity on your values, make a list, and align them with your activities. Once you know what your values are, let them guide your actions in everyday life.

My values are (circle 10):

Affection	Genuineness	Recognition
Alignment	Happiness	Respect
Altruism	Harmony	Results
Appearance	Health	Routine
Appreciated	Honesty	Romance
Attitude	Humility	Security
Cleanliness	Inner Peace	See The World
Congruence	Inspiration	Simplicity
Contentment	Intimacy	Solitude
Cooperation	Joy	Spiritual Maturity
Creativity	Knowledge	Status
Education	Lifestyle	Wealth
Effectiveness	Loyalty	Winning
Efficiency	Loved	Wisdom
Fairness	Motivation	
Faith	Openness	
Fame	Organization	
Family	Personal Brand	
Financial Security	Personal Improvement	
Freedom	Personal Salvation	
Friendship	Philanthropy	
Fun	Power	
Generosity	Productivity	

Once you understand what your values are, assess your life and businesses and see if your actions actually match your values. Documenting your values help to identify areas where change is necessary and it makes future decisions simple and clear.

Think back to what you've done in the last 24 hours and write down the activities and times. Now take your list of values and match each activity back to one of your values. Some activities may connect strongly to one or more of your values, while others will be a stretch. Some may not support your values at all. Those are the ones you can discard.

When your behavior conflicts with your values, the result is a mental conflict. Psychologists call this cognitive dissonance and it is a source of pain and stress in your life.

When you have focus, then it's time to use the power of visualization to make your goals a reality. Remember, your goals will become reality faster with less stress if they follow and are aligned with your values.

> **WHEN YOUR VALUES ARE CLEAR, YOUR DECISIONS BECOME EASIER.**
> **–PETER THOMAS**

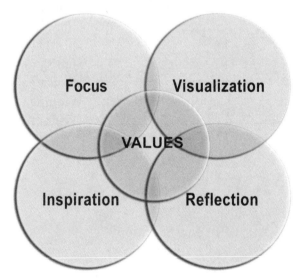

I (Peter) took my helicopter course years ago and there are several gauges you have to know how to use to fly. It was absolutely essential to learn how to operate those gauges because when you hit a storm, you live by those gauges. What will you do when you hit the storm? Learn how to focus on your values now, so you can live by them in all seasons and avoid the pitfalls in life.

My values center on health, freedom, happiness, and integrity. When I hit patches of chaos, I refer back to my core values.

We've both known guys who get into trouble, and then they cave. They turn to alcohol, affairs, or some other addiction to handle stress. They stop running or exercising, stop their habits of success, and start going off the deep end. That's because they didn't have a plan for the tough times and they get derailed.

This doesn't have to be your fate. Know your values and keep your focus.

22.
You Can't Get Where You're Going Without a Plan

Success is very seldom about pure luck. We are successful when we achieve objectives on purpose. In other words, we have thought through our vision, are clear on what we want to achieve, and then systematically go about taking the actions that will get us where we want to go. In a nutshell, this is what planning is about. If you don't create a plan, it's almost impossible to achieve your vision.

Having a mission statement (the why) and a set of goals or objectives (the targets) are important (both personal and business) in order to achieve the right results faster. Every entrepreneur needs a clean and current action plan. If you don't have one, you're simply costing yourself time and money, living your business life on autopilot. That's not a way to operate.

Your plan should be a values-based strategy for the long haul. By values-based, we mean that it's critical to establish clarity about what matters most to you first as the leader, and then create your vision, mission, and objectives from your values.

Remember the great explorers Christopher Columbus and Lewis and Clark? They had a vision. They had a plan. A plan will help you navigate treacherous waters,

> GO AS FAR AS YOU CAN SEE, THEN YOU CAN SEE FARTHER.
> –TONY JEARY

or avoid them altogether, and help keep you focused. Clear vision is critical to success and effectiveness so it is easy to understand why vision is critical when you understand what success really is. We are successful when we achieve objectives we have established in advance. And how will we establish them? With a plan.

23.
Make a Life List

I (Tony) grew up amazed at many of the things my dad was able to accomplish. He could fix just about anything, he knew everybody, and he made lists for everything. My dad has served people all his life, and every day I think of him and how he has impacted me and my success through these simple things—serving, connecting, and list-making.

Just last week he, my mother, and brother came to our home in Dallas for a visit. I was up early working out and asked my dad to join me. He watched. I trained. Afterwards we went to the kitchen table to visit. Guess what he pulled out of his pocket? That's right: a list. It was hand written, organized, and focused. I loved it!

One of the most powerful habits that lead to successful accelerated results is the list. That's right—making lists and checking them more than twice. But a list is not just about business; it's about the fun things you want to do with your family, your friends, and your life as well. It's even about your health (read *Ultimate Health*, Carpenter and Son, 2013).

In the rubble of 9/11, a computer was discovered in the wreckage that held a life list of one hundred things a girl wanted to do before she died. Her parents found some comfort in knowing she had achieved quite a few of them.

Make a Life List today of the one hundred things you want to do before you die. Some people call it the bucket list. It should contain places you want to travel, people you want to meet, things you want

> GET CLEAR ON WHAT YOU WANT TO HAVE, SHARE, EXPERIENCE, AND PERHAPS MOST IMPORTANTLY, WHAT YOU WANT TO BECOME.
> –TONY JEARY

to see, and items you want to own. This list isn't magical, but it's a dream list that you can turn into reality, with focus. Writing the list is the first step toward giving your goals the focused attention they deserve.

24.
Design Your Own Life

Think of yourself as an architect. You can build whatever you want. To have the life you want, it needs to be designed. When you design your own life, you have a vision, a plan, and a schematic of how things look. The alternative is to let other people or circumstances design a life for you.

Designing your own life is different than making a Life List or bucket list (see #23). A list is just a list. Designing something indicates action. It is fluid and ongoing as you create what you'd like your life to be.

WHEN YOU DESIGN YOUR OWN LIFE, YOU HAVE A VISION, A PLAN, AND A SCHEMATIC OF HOW THINGS LOOK.

Think about the rest of your life and what you would like to accomplish. Some examples of goals might be to write a book, run for public office, climb a mountain, or learn a foreign language. Write down some long-term goals or dreams. Edit or refer to them constantly. (Build yourself a literal and electronic binder, and keep detailing it the rest of your life.) Where will you live in five years? What will your homes look like? Craft a plan for each decade. How do you want things to look at forty or fifty? What about sixty or seventy? When you're eighty, where will you live, how healthy do you plan to be, and how will you spend your free time?

So many times we see people set extravagant goals, such as, "Once I build my company and sell it I'm going to go live on an island." That's a big, bold statement and a fun goal, but it's often better to set small motivations and enjoy life within certain terms. Design your life so that you are motivated to achieve through a process of clarity, planning, visualization, and reward. What motivates you? We reward ourselves with trips, experiences, free time, and brief sabbaticals in special places.

When I (Peter) was sixteen years old, I left home and joined the Canadian Army. For the first two of seven years, we went to school just like other kids; the only difference was that we wore the uniform and went to sleep in the barracks like other soldiers. After we had finished our basic training we were allowed to have weekend and evening passes, and a lot of freedom.

> REMEMBER, CLARITY PULLS YOU TOWARD THE RESULTS YOU ENVISION.
> –TONY JEARY

I was a bit of a loner and headed for the nearest city, Barrie, Ontario, where I met lots of people and found a girlfriend. However, some of the people were not the best friends for me to choose. One night we were out in a car driving around. All of a sudden, the driver stopped the car on a city street and jumped out, as did the fellow in the front seat with him. I did not pay much attention until I heard the sound of metal and I immediately recognized that they were stealing the hubcaps from a parked car. Instantly, a scene of me being taken away to jail for stealing and being kicked out of the army came to my mind. That was not how I wanted to design my life! I crawled out of the back seat and ran down the street away from that car and those people as fast as my legs could take me.

The purpose of telling you this story is to remind you that you and you alone have the power of choice. I exercised my power of choice when it would have been easier to go along with the guys stealing hubcaps. Without fail, we will come to a cross roads at some point in our lives—maybe several times—and it is the choices we make at these times that often define our destinies.

Life is a series of choices; you cannot blame anyone else for the choices you make. When you design your own life, remember to make the right choices each day. Choices will impact your future, and your success is up to you.

25.
Utilize the Power
of Visualization

High achievers get results because they know what they want and they execute a plan to get it. But before they do any execution, they visualize the result.

Successful people create a tangible vision that motivates them toward what they desire to achieve. They understand how important it is to engage the visual aspect of motivating themselves and their teams toward their goals. Visualization is a key aspect of becoming a winner and achieving exactly what you want.

Remember that clarity pulls you toward the outcome and the results you envision (see #20). There is a pulling power to clarity that guides entrepreneurs to achieve their dreams and goals.

> VISUALIZATION IS A KEY ASPECT OF BECOMING A WINNER AND ACHIEVING EXACTLY WHAT YOU WANT.

But it is not enough to just have a goal. Ridiculously successful people are very clear and specific about their goals. How? They utilize visualization techniques.

One technique is to create a vision board of your goals. Cut out photos of what you want and post them for you to see daily. This continual reminder is a powerful trigger. Another technique is to create a list of what you want more of and less of in life (see #30).

Both of us have used powerful visualization in our lives for decades by seeing the goal we want before it's achieved. For years, I (Tony) have helped people improve their thinking and use tools to create mastery in their lives and businesses. I have a vision wall that I look at daily, with inspiring images of goals and also goals I've attained. This vision wall includes pictures of family vacations, my kids' events, and business achievements. I encourage you to start practicing the power of visualization today by taking several hours to create images of the goals you want to achieve. (Google Tony Jeary on "Results Boarding" for a powerful video on the topic.)

When I (Peter) started selling mutual funds many years ago, I was reading a business magazine and in it was a picture of a Lear Jet. It was the most beautiful thing I had ever seen, and I knew in my heart that I wanted one. I cut the picture out of the magazine and put it up on the wall directly across from my desk. Six years later, I actually owned that jet.

> VISUALIZATION IS THE ABILITY TO "SEE" THE END RESULT BEFORE YOU BEGIN.
>
> –PETER THOMAS

The power of visualization is one of the most powerful motivating tools you will ever have. What are the things you are visualizing into reality? Get clear on what you want to have, share, and most importantly what you want to become. In a world full of distractions, we need constant triggers and visual markers to keep us on track and focused, similar to how highways have signs that mark the right way to go to get to your destination.

26.
Pause to Reflect

Computers, cars, and airplanes come with operating manuals. Human beings don't. Most of what we know is based on trial and error and how much we are willing and able to learn from others. When we first enter the world, much of our focus is spent on just staying physically upright, and satisfying our basic needs for food, love, comfort, and warmth. We feel our way through our early years, guided by a combination of nature and nurture.

As we grow, our needs become far more complex. Before we know it, it's not about keeping our balance as we learn to walk or ride a bike—it's about trying to cope with balancing our businesses and our entire lives. How are you doing at this right now? How would you rate yourself?

With no operating manual to guide you, it's not surprising so many wind up feeling off-balance, unfulfilled, or just plain lost. Many rush from one task to another like they're living on a treadmill. We reach for certain successes, only to achieve them and perhaps discover they aren't as satisfying as we hoped they'd be. Does it ever seem like there's never enough time for all the things that really matter?

> REFLECTION IS THE BRIDGE BETWEEN YOUR EXPERIENCES AND YOUR LEARNING.
> - PETER THOMAS

Pause for a moment and take stock of where you are and where you've been (both business and personal). Self-awareness and, therefore, self-analysis are cornerstones of Emotional Intelligence. Socrates said, "The unexamined life is not worth living." A bit severe, but he was probably onto something.

So, why reflect? Why bother? Why not simply forge ahead and believe that what is behind you should remain there? Reflection is the bridge between your experiences and your learning. The aim here is to review, to understand, to discover, to examine your lessons, and then to engrave this wisdom on your present and future.

Another great benefit of reflection is that of celebration! Busy and ambitious leaders, especially, find themselves barreling through goals, impatiently leaping from endeavor to conquest, and rarely investing any time acknowledging their accomplishments. But why achieve all these things if you don't take time to reflect on a job well done?

Reflection permits you to log your successes and capitalize on your challenges and tests in life. Revisiting your achievements is a great exercise to do with your team. Assessing what you have gained from strategic plans and decisions is a powerful tool for further growth.

Ultimately, if you wish to live and lead by your values, how else can you check up on yourself along the way? Pause and look back to see how far you've come. Make it a standard to do this often.

27.
Develop a Likeness Matrix

Successful people set goals and utilize visualization. They even do vision boards (see #25). To go to another level, let us introduce you to the "likeness matrix." I (Tony) share this tool with many of my top clients and give further emphasis on the power of clarity. Here's how it works.

Subject	Example	Distinctions	How

For instance, when I travel to Vegas we stay at the Encore. The way Steve keeps the property manicured is the way I want my estate manicured. So I take pictures and show my gardeners. Therefore on my "likeness matrix," I have this as a standard.

A few years back, I visited Joel Katz, the famous attorney who helped

> **SUCCESSFUL PEOPLE SET GOALS AND UTILIZE VISUALIZATION.**

> **CREATE AND CONTINUE TO CREATE "WOW MOMENTS" FOR OTHERS AND FOR YOURSELF.**
> **–PETER THOMAS**

invent Margaritaville with Jimmy Buffet. We met in his office for five hours and I was so impressed with the concierge-type approach his staff plays out with anyone in his office. So on our likeness matrix, we have a standard to have our team create a "wow"-type experience when anyone visits my studio or office. We clean their cars and surprise them, we serve health shakes, we keep fresh fruit around, we have extra iPads lying around, and we take pictures and build memory boards for visitors and clients.

Develop a list of things you want to model. To be really clear, review it, take pictures, take video, and really determine what you want things to be like, including how you treat your customers, how you keep your business clean, how you run your operation—even down to how to keep your vehicles, home, and closet.

Get extremely clear and specific. Make your business and life what you want it to be.

III. TIME

*"I'm here to build something for the long-term.
Anything else is a distraction."*
– MARK ZUCKERBERG

*"Yesterday is gone. Tomorrow has not yet come.
We have only today. Let us begin."*
- MOTHER TERESA

*"The future is something which everyone reaches at the rate of sixty
minutes an hour, whatever he does, whoever he is."*
- C.S. LEWIS

28.
Say "No" Often

In today's fast-paced world, we are presented with opportunities almost every waking minute. Services, messages, products, emails, phone calls, offers, meetings, and activities bombard us on a continual basis. We are possibilities people, so sometimes these things look attractive. But it is possible to have too many choices. Say no to the things that don't matter the most. That's the magical rule. It takes discipline and good thinking to a whole different level.

> **WHEN YOU SAY YES, YOU'RE SAYING NO TO SOMETHING ELSE.**

People don't say no because they don't know how, they don't want to miss out on anything, or they don't want to offend someone. But people-pleasers are rarely wildly successful entrepreneurs. If you don't learn how to say no, needless activities can pile up on the calendar, draining valuable moments from important projects and goals—valuable moments from your life that you'll never get back.

So many people say yes and get into messes, partnerships, deals, and relationships because they didn't say no at the right time. Most often the right time to say no is at the beginning.

Say no strategically. There are a lot of ways to say no and make people feel as if you still care. If you're an author, for instance, you can say no to a free speech opportunity and offer to send them a free case of your books for their group or event. If you're an entrepreneur who gets invited to participate in a deal, you can say no and send one of your colleagues to the meeting instead and to do the research.

When you say yes, you're saying no to something else. When you say yes to a client dinner, for instance, you could be saying no to dinner with your children. When you say yes to counseling someone after work, you could be saying no to counseling a family member in your own home. When you say yes to lunch with a friend, you might be saying no to an important deadline getting completed at the office. If you say yes to every activity, meeting, lunch, or volunteer opportunity, you're saying no to anything else that could have been in that time slot. It is easier to build relationships and build your business when you eliminate so many of the distractions, unwanted attention, unnecessary obligations, and meaningless meetings.

> TAKE TIME FOR
> REFLECTION,
> INTROSPECTION, AND
> STILLNESS. TAKE THE
> TIME TO BLOCK OUT THE
> WORLD AND BE WITH
> YOURSELF.
> –PETER THOMAS

Saying no is empowering. It helps build your self-esteem, reduces stress, and gives you more time and energy. Successful businesses are not built on a feeling of obligation or a fear of saying no. Successful businesses are built when clarity, focus, and execution converge over and over again.

It also creates space. In order to create margin time, which is that extra space in your life that you very rarely have, you have to start getting good at saying no more often. Even if it's just a moment of solitude, the time you create is better than engaging in something you didn't want to be a part of in the first place.

29.
Manage Time (Don't Let Time Manage You)

When it comes to business, winning, and defeating the competition, we need to realize that everyone has the same amount of time to begin with. How we utilize that time can make the difference in winning and losing. Do you value your time? And will you use it to build a competitive advantage?

Avoid time and energy wasters—those distractions and people that suck both time and joy right out of your day. Detox your life from anyone who isn't good for you, or wastes your time, distracting you from your goals. A lack of discipline and poor habits are indicators of a lack of success, and unsuccessful people don't want the other person to win. Often, these people are time wasters with a lot to say; and if you allow them to, they will talk incessantly about their problems, their lack of business, or the conflict that they're having with friends or family. Before you know it, you've missed a deadline or an important business meeting, or you've given up hours that could have been spent on something valuable.

> **THE KEY TO GOOD TIME MANAGEMENT AND EMOTIONAL HEALTH IS TO BE PROACTIVE, NOT REACTIVE.**

Managing time also means managing your emotions. I (Peter) have found over the years that I am very active and very alert, with my radar always on. In several instances, this has proved not to be good, especially at airports. I used to get very caught up in some of the ridiculous situations that occur when taking a flight. After a particularly bad experience in some international location where our bags were lost and no one seemed to care, I decided to learn a way to de-stress myself and gracefully cope with whatever issues come up, rather than getting so worked up that it ruined my day and affected the moods of those traveling with me.

I took a self-hypnosis course from Dr. Lee Pulos, a friend and a fantastic teacher. He taught me how to take myself "down" so I invented what I called my Zone One, Zone Two, and Zone Three. These Zones represented levels of activity and emotion. Zone One was fully alert and highly sensitive—my normal condition; Zone Two was slowed down considerably, more observant than reactive; and Zone Three was almost comatose.

> THERE ARE 168 HOURS IN A WEEK. YOU SLEEP 56 AND DO MAINTENANCE FOR 12; THAT LEAVES 100 HOURS. MANAGE THOSE HOURS WELL!
> –TONY JEARY

I decided that I would let my wife handle all logistics and I would go into Zone Three as soon as I got into the airport. It has worked perfectly! It has been a long time since I have let an airport stress me out and I guarantee you that my wife and travel companions appreciate this as well.

What you do with your time matters. People can either multiply your time or waste it. They can accelerate your emotions or soothe them. The key to good time management and emotional health is to be proactive, not reactive.

30.
MOLO Your Life
(More of, Less of)

What do you want more of in life? In business? In your relations? What do you want less of?

Most people look at conducting a MOLO (more of, less of) exercise as something you do for an entity, or for an organization, not an individual. But being able to utilize this as a leadership tool allows you to ensure you're detecting where your opportunities truly are, and that you are capitalizing on your strengths, efforts, time, and resources.

Make lists for what you want more of, and what you want less of. MOLO forces you to continually think of what you want to keep and what you want to eliminate, much like the vision (results) boarding exercise (see #25). Consider posting lists in a visible place in your house and offices so that you see them every day. Keep MOLO in the forefront of your mind. Focus on the things you want more of like health, deals, fun clients, or other business contacts so they will be drawn into your world. The more focus, the more draw. The things you want less of will help you best route energies elsewhere.

> **FOCUS ON THE THINGS YOU WANT MORE OF SO THEY WILL BE DRAWN INTO YOUR WORLD.**

Omit the things you don't want out of your business and life. Get rid of them. Get rid of things that complicate and clutter. Many know what they want more of, but few strategically think much on eliminating things like excess meetings, recourse debt, toxic people, or even things

> NO ONE HAS ENOUGH TIME, YET EVERYONE HAS ALL THERE IS. WHAT WE DO WITH OUR TIME DETERMINES WHAT WE ACCOMPLISH WITH OUR LIVES.
>
> –TONY JEARY

like conflict.

We say eliminate every negative, if you can. Suppose someone gave you an object you loathe, and you feel irritated—even just for a second—each time you see it. Sure, it's only one second or two, and you feel obligated to keep the item, but over the course of a year, that's a lot of seconds that bring you negative feelings. Why would you keep it? This is a small example of a big principle. Don't say yes when you mean no, and don't live with things you don't like. Don't allow things in your business that drag morale down, pull happiness away, or even just cause undue stress.

If you focus on eliminating friction every day, you will dramatically impact your life. What do you want to stop doing, start doing, or do differently? Audit yourself, your team, your whole organization, and determine what you need to do more of, less of, or do differently. Start doing or stop doing. This rule is one of the most impactful things I've (Tony) coached Peter on and he shares this knowledge with all those around him.

31.
Create Elegant Solutions

An *Elegant Solution* is when you are so clear on your objectives that you can accomplish more than one thing at a time by combining them. It's a powerful way of prioritizing and maximizing your time. Ask yourself if you're really clear on your vision, where you're going, and what your goals and objectives are. Are your goals and objectives in front of you where you can be reminded of them every day? When you do, you will continually think of ways to create Elegant Solutions and accomplish several objectives at one time.

> AN *ELEGANT SOLUTION* IS BEING SO CLEAR ON YOUR GOALS, OBJECTIVES, AND PRIORITIES THAT YOU CAN DO ONE THING AND ACCOMPLISH MULTIPLE OBJECTIVES AT THE SAME TIME.
> –TONY JEARY

One example of an Elegant Solution that I (Tony) really like is to have fitness-based meetings. For clients who have the same goal of maintaining physical fitness as I do, I invite them over to my gym to work out, talk, and generate ideas on a flipchart. One positive outcome is that that two-hour block of time is spent in the gym working out. Another outcome is that I can talk about business with my clients. Another positive result of that Elegant Solution is that a staff member or colleague is normally taking notes, interjecting ideas, or capturing what's going on. Elegant Solutions create wins for everyone involved.

Another example would be providing personal and business value to your clients at the same time or conducting more efficient meetings.

Consider taking a valued client or colleague out for a day of golf where you have an opportunity to show appreciation on a personal level, but at the same time you solidify relationships and have a chance throughout the day to discuss business opportunities as well.

In order to maximize my time, I've had a driver for twenty years who drives me to meetings so I can do business in the backseat, take notes, read, and conduct conference calls—all because I don't have to drive.

Examples of Elegant Solutions:
- Invite someone you're mentoring (or perhaps a new team member) to participate in a meeting that would add value to them and teach them simultaneously.
- Take your kids on a business trip with you to help them learn and spend time together while you're working.
- Plan a business lunch or happy hour at a popular networking spot to perhaps connect with others at the same time.
- Select places to vacation where your family can learn a new culture or experience something new, while also spending quality time together. Talk about your goals on the trip.
- Host an event that both brings value to your clients but also connects them with others who can bring value to them.
- Work out with a business colleague or client.

CREATING ELEGANT SOLUTIONS LEADS TO MULTIPLE WINS.

Creating Elegant Solutions leads to multiple wins. What you do with your time determines what you do with your life. Begin to rethink your time habits and better understand how the time investment choices you make really affect the results you seek. Then, work to create elegant solutions that allow you to accomplish more in the same amount of time.

32.
Understand Positive and Negative Procrastination

Let's face it—we all procrastinate sometimes. But you can't produce results until you start doing something. There are two kinds of procrastination: positive and negative. Positive procrastination can be beneficial, whereas negative procrastination just impedes production and therefore results. An example of positive procrastination is when you legitimately need some "mental percolation" time to gather your thoughts. Negative procrastination is based on a flimsy excuse to avoid doing something now.

> LIVE *PRODUCTION BEFORE PERFECTION.* THE MAIN IDEA OF (PBP) IS TO ACT FIRST, AND GET IT PERFECT LATER. OPERATING WITH A PBP MINDSET HELPS US FLOW MUCH MORE EFFECTIVELY IN THE FAST-PACED WORLD WE LIVE IN TODAY.
> –TONY JEARY

Production Before Perfection (PBP) is the self-talk that says it doesn't have to be perfect to get it going; get it going and perfect it along the way (see #91). It's my solution to negative procrastination. Let me repeat—you can't produce results until you start doing something, right? If you do nothing, that is exactly what you'll get—nothing. If you do something, the possibilities are endless.

Just a warning: When you start to practice PBP, you will be doing things in a way that conflicts with the thinking of 90 percent of people on this planet, so be ready to encounter resistance. It is not the natural thing to do, and you will have to hear and overcome objections on why you should wait. But waiting and getting results are not compatible. If you wait, you burn time you cannot get back. The same goes for your team and your entire organization.

People who use planning to avoid action often get tangled in an unhealthy emotional cycle of evaluation and analysis paralysis. Preparation and planning are important, but excessive preparation is nothing more than procrastination – it's that simple. It is only when you start doing what you need to do that you can begin to produce results. Sometimes the best way to manage your emotions is to ignore them and keep pushing through to achieve what it is you need to do. If you procrastinate, it means you are fearful of failure and may not be confident in your ability to succeed. This is when self-talk and what you say to yourself becomes extremely important.

WHEN YOU QUIT IN THE FACE OF ADVERSITY, IT MEANS YOU ARE DEFICIENT IN THE MENTAL SUBSTANCE IT TAKES TO PERSEVERE AND OVERCOME.

People who quit too easily or give up in the face of adversity generate a complex chain of emotions and events that negatively impact their mind, hence their business results. It is always easy to quit, and too many people prefer quitting to the discomfort they experience when the going gets tough. The reason is simple: Adversity is painful. When you quit in the face of adversity, it means you are deficient in the mental substance it takes to persevere and overcome.

Go as far as you can see, and then you'll see farther. This concept has the power to nip procrastination in the bud before it has a chance to flower. You don't always have to understand all the details between where you are and where you want to be. You simply have to forge ahead, despite any resistance or desire to procrastinate. Your success is right around the corner.

IV. STRATEGIC

"Always look for the fool in the deal. If you don't find one, it's you."
– MARK CUBAN

"Never interrupt your enemy when he is making a mistake."
- NAPOLEON BONAPARTE

"In preparing for battle I have always found that plans are useless, but planning is indispensable."
- DWIGHT D. EISENHOWER

33.
Be Intentional About Everything

Intentionality is different than clarity or focus. Intentionality comes from the root of your intention. It centers not just around thought, but action. Be intentional about who you spend time with. Hang around others who match your values. Be intentional about every action.

It all starts with clarity (see #20). When you are in tune with your values and you know the values you live by, you become intentional about every aspect of your life.

> WHEN YOU ARE IN TUNE WITH YOUR VALUES AND YOU KNOW THE VALUES YOU LIVE BY, YOU BECOME INTENTIONAL ABOUT EVERY ASPECT OF YOUR LIFE.

In business, you should have set standards for what you want and what you don't want, well thought out and documented. If a big part of your success is the people around you, then replace those who aren't right for you with some who are.

Be intentional about how much stress you can manage, how many projects you can take on, and why. Don't do things without thinking. Think. Be strategic, then do things fast and your energy and resources will be expended and utilized in the best way.

What we value in ourselves and what others appreciate about us often relate to our self-esteem. Take time to identify the qualities and characteristics you like about yourself—your natural talents and strengths. When you take time to think about and identify your values, you become much more intentional.

BE BOTH STRATEGIC
AND INTENTIONAL
ABOUT EVERY SINGLE
THING YOU DO.
–TONY JEARY

Intentionality exists when you know exactly what you want, and everything flows from that. First, you must know what you really want. Then you can be intentional about taking action.

34.
Establish the Rules Before You Start the Game

Negotiation is the key to success in getting what you want in a deal. If you negotiate effectively, you establish the rules up front and you're aware of the playing field. Not everything can be predicted, of course, but you can certainly do your due diligence and communicate expectations so that everyone is aware of them ahead of time. Unmet or unrealized expectations can kill success, so establish them up front, and make sure everyone buys in.

When I (Peter) do a franchise deal for Dogtopia, my latest franchise interest, I make sure we have all the rules of the game laid out on paper so that the franchisee understands the level of their commitment.

Strategic Acceleration, which is what Tony teaches, helps entrepreneurs get clarity and focus on things that need to be done. Communication Mastery, one of Tony's strategies, provides the methodology and the means by which those things can be communicated throughout the organization. The point is to teach people to elevate their communication skills, so that everyone gets more clarity, additional focus, and even greater ability to execute consistently.

It is important to remember that every deal and every organization is comprised of people whose success depends on their collective abilities. No matter how large or small your organization is, communication

> **EVERY DEAL AND EVERY ORGANIZATION IS COMPRISED OF PEOPLE WHOSE SUCCESS DEPENDS ON THEIR COLLECTIVE ABILITIES.**

has to be clear in order to have impact and get results. Does your team understand the rules of the game? Do the people you're doing business with understand what the objective is, how to measure progress, and what will occur if the deal falls through or someone wants out? When you communicate the rules in advance, you prevent misunderstandings and pitfalls. It's as simple as that.

Communicate, communicate, and then communicate more!

35.
Use the Tools That Give You Leverage

Having the right tools at the right time can make a world of difference.

Most people don't really understand that if they have an arsenal of tools, they'll execute faster. Most people work harder and put their own internal team under more stress because they're constantly meeting, sending out sales emails, trying to get prospective buyers, and responding to leads. But you don't have to be like most people.

When you have tools, you already have the response ready. You are taking a proactive approach. Tools can help you sell, raise money, and manage and lead people. You don't have to recreate the wheel to buy, lease, or attract a big toolbox.

Create an arsenal you can send to clients as well. In our office, we create books, DVDs, book recaps, and even goal setting or business plan templates that we give away to clients to help them win. We give people tools that will help them succeed at business, team building, development, or strategy. When they win, we win.

As a leader, you should have a big toolbox for your organization. If you don't know where to start to create your toolbox, make a list of the things people want from you. Instead of recreating the wheel, develop a tool mindset. Do you need an app? Do you need a book? What tools do your competitors have that you don't?

To be more valuable as an entrepreneur or as any kind of leader, we recommend you build an arsenal of tools you can use to provide value to others and to help you present your messaging. That means setting up a system, both for yourself and your team, that you can use to catalog and organize items of value and content, and build your own research toolbox.

> **HAVING THE RIGHT TOOLS AT THE RIGHT TIME CAN MAKE A WORLD OF DIFFERENCE.**

An arsenal can be in the form of a list of helpful URLs or videos, powerful books, summaries, whitepapers, examples, case studies, photographs, animations, and more. Just like a military arsenal, the idea is to "arm" you in your business to respond quickly. The real concept is that little by little, week by week, month by month, you're building an intentional arsenal. That arsenal can sometimes be leveraged down. You can even have others maintain it for you.

Utilizing an Internet site where appropriate is one way to utilize your arsenal. The key is that it becomes more powerful based on the friendliness and retrievability of the content. The more robust your arsenal, the better equipped you will be to respond to every situation.

36.
Initially Structure the Partnership Properly

If you feel a partnership in any venture is the right move, leave nothing to chance. Structure the partnership with all the "what if's" in mind. In business, you don't get what you deserve—you get what you negotiate. We've all heard and know this. Have an agreement in place and know your exit options up front—how you will get out (or how someone else will get out) from day one, if that time ever comes. Think ahead to all the possibilities.

> **BUDGET FOR STRATEGY FIRST; IT MATTERS THE MOST.**
> **–TONY JEARY**

Let's say you start a partnership with a friend. The business is successful and thrives. Twenty years later, your friend wants to retire but you don't. What happens now? Have a plan in place for all the possibilities so there's no question. Use an expert (or whole team) to put the plan in place and have all parties sign off so there are no misunderstandings down the line. Include things like divorce, lawsuits, if children want to buy in, if you need more capital—cover the most common "what if's."

37.
Watch for the Warning Signs

Before any deal crashes, there are signs. A bad real estate market doesn't just happen overnight, for instance. There are always signs, and if you can see them early, you might just be able to avoid trouble. If it's a real estate project and the lots aren't selling, ask yourself why. Detect deficiencies. Recognize early on when you are in trouble so you don't lose your decision-making ability. Cut your losses and don't feed a bad deal. Most don't get better.

> **THERE ARE ALWAYS SIGNS, AND IF YOU CAN SEE THEM EARLY, YOU MIGHT JUST BE ABLE TO AVOID TROUBLE.**

Ask yourself, "Is this deal headed for success?" And, "What's the best use of my time right now?" These questions will help raise your self-awareness and help you to understand your motives and actions for doing what you do, and will also identify bad habits or weaknesses in your business, or in yourself. Continually examine your deals and activities and watch for any signs of weakness or areas for improvement. Be willing to move on.

Take time to evaluate, and pay attention to the warning signs. Then act accordingly.

38.
Know the Rules
of Negotiation

In order to understand the rules of negotiation, you really have to understand what negotiation really is. It's not just talking and determining what you want and how you're going to get it. Negotiation is about making things happen by understanding what other people want. Remember, you win when they win. But if you think they want something other than what they really want, you will address the wrong points and miss the mark.

Have you ever met someone who talks over everyone? That person doesn't win because they don't carefully listen to the other side of the story. They're also not a good negotiator because they are only focused on themselves, and negotiation is a balance of give and take.

It all starts with other people's interest. Do your homework, and dis-

> **NEGOTIATION IS ABOUT MAKING THINGS HAPPEN BY UNDERSTANDING WHAT OTHER PEOPLE WANT.**

cover everything in advance about the other party—their motivations, promotions, and timing. Knowledge is power. Once you understand their position and priorities, you can implement your powers of persuasion to make an impact and often more easily persuade them to your thinking.

It's not about winning at all costs. Some people want to win no matter what, even at the expense of everyone else; but inevitably, that will cost you in the long run. You don't have to be everyone's friend in the world, either. However, you don't need to make enemies. You never know when you might need the person you're trying to negotiate with, or where your next deal will come from. It may be a friend of the person you want to say no to. It's best to leave a good impression every time.

Have people leave your office happy. When you must say no, have them feel like you said yes. Look for alternatives. The true art of negotiation is when you can help make everyone win.

39.
Stay Competitive

High achievers have to know what's going on with their competitors. That doesn't mean you have to spend mental energy on knowing what your competition is doing day-to-day; however, as a successful professional, it's important to know how your competitors are talking to your existing clients or prospects. What are they saying about you? What are they saying about your business? Do they have an online footprint that you don't have?

Successful people keep up with changing technology to remain competitive, and that includes social media. But, as with everything, there's a balance. A lot of people are making a lot of money with face-to-face contact, and a lot of people are losing money because they're completely focused on social media and not on face-to-face relationships. Do your due diligence and know where your Blind Spots are (see #3). Stay competitive on the ground and stay competitive in virtual spaces.

> YOU MAY NOT NEED THE LATEST ADVANCES IN TECHNOLOGY. HOWEVER, ONE THING IS FOR SURE: YOU WILL NEED WHATEVER IT IS THAT YOUR CUSTOMERS WANT.

You can make a small business seem like a medium or large size business by harnessing the power of technology. One way is to utilize email contact databases. Successful people build a database of existing clients and customers and then they drip value and market to them year after year for repeat business. Email blasts, text marketing, and other ways of communicating virtually and not just through social media sites like LinkedIn or Facebook can help you stay in touch with your customers and communicate vital messages.

You may not need the latest advances in technology. However, one thing is for sure: You will need whatever it is that your customers want. If you're still using LinkedIn or Facebook five years from now and your customer is using a completely different method of social media to communicate with people, you could be missing out. It's no different than talking to your spouse in a way he or she does not comprehend.

Leverage the power of technology in your business to strengthen relationships with clients. Set up specific systems so that you have a method for automatically generating a message with new information to clients systematically. In this mobile world, technology makes it simple to foster stronger relationships; and if you're not using it, you're losing.

40.
Rewarding Yourself
Often Creates Inspiration
and Motivation

Rewarding yourself is a great way to feel satisfaction about the things you're achieving and inspire yourself to do more. Pay yourself first. Buy a nice car, enjoy your hard work, take well planned vacations. We say the more vacations you take, the more money you make.

> KEEP THE REWARD IN FOCUS, BECAUSE IT WILL INSPIRE YOU TO WORK HARDER.

Rewards can also be small things like sharing a concert with a friend, having a special date night, or purchasing a new gadget—anything that feels like a treat or reward to you. If you do these things you'll be much less likely to be burned out because you will see the value in what you are working to achieve and what you're building, making your vision a reality.

We've all seen it—some people go years without a vacation only to find themselves burned out, stressed out, and unable to move forward. These are often the people who get so stuck that they don't want to do what they're doing anymore. They've worked so hard without a reward, only to find that they've lost their passion.

Ask yourself, "Do I keep rewards strategically in front of me to continually motivate and inspire me to reach my goals?" If not, you can start today.

Maybe it's a vision board or a picture of a new vehicle (see #25), or perhaps it's a trip that you already have booked on the calendar. Whatever it is, keep the reward in focus, because it will inspire you to work harder, and keep on keeping on. And let's face it, we enjoy knowing that there's a reward coming soon.

41.
Move from Great to Mastery in All You Do

We all know that good just isn't good enough anymore, but what if you could strive to go beyond great? Great is a high standard, but an even higher standard would be to become the expert in your field. There's a quarterback, and then there's the best quarterback in the nation. There's a runner, and then there's the runner with the fastest time. You don't have to make it an all-out competition with everyone else, but you should strive to become the master in your particular line of business. It's about being better than you already are and achieving a level of mastery that others will notice.

What is mastery? The simple definition means "control or superiority over" something else. It doesn't mean winning at the expense of others, but it sets you apart from others who have become content with the status quo.

STRIVE TO BECOME THE MASTER IN YOUR PARTICULAR LINE OF BUSINESS.

Mostly, mastery is about rising above contentment if you find that you're no longer growing your thinking, yourself, or your business. Although there is no scientific information to support it, I believe less than 5 percent of people live and work in mastery.

What are the characteristics of those 5-percenters? They are big-picture thinkers and think outside the box. They consistently ask themselves if there is a better or faster way to accomplish the same result. Once they've accomplished a goal, they ask what's next. They take initiative, and they're resilient. They are self-motivated and they believe that there is a way to accomplish things that haven't been done before. They are results-driven and are willing to work harder and smarter than others. They are relationship nurturers. They accept nothing short of excellence, and they are focused on continuous improvement - not because of lack of contentment but because they don't want to settle for less than the best.

Examine your business and your habits. Are there any areas, concerns, or situations that are preventing you from achieving mastery? Do you operate at the mastery level and create superior results in every area of your life?

Strive for a higher level of success and make mastery your goal. A big part of becoming the master at something is how well you execute in order to achieve results. You can say the right things, do the right things, and even look the right way. But if you're not achieving results for people, you're not providing value. Seek mastery in everything that you do, and value will be a natural result.

42.
Live in Solutions:
Be Strategic vs. Tactical

The most successful people don't dwell on problems - they live in solutions. We all know that change happens fast and often without warning, and that problems do exist. But change can also create opportunities to provide solutions to problems. It's all about perspective.

What do you do when change hits and problems arise? It's human nature to hunker down, cling to the status quo, and hope the storm passes. Even if the end result isn't negative, most people see change as a threat that will require them to move outside their comfort zone and learn and think differently. Learning and thinking in new ways can be a real challenge sometimes, especially when under pressure or stress.

> **THE MORE YOU LIVE IN SOLUTIONS, THE MORE NATURALLY STRATEGIC YOU'LL BECOME.**

But thinking strategically and focusing on solutions rather than problems is the mindset you need, especially during times of change. When you think strategically, you are thinking about how to exploit change as a positive resource, rather than dwelling on a perceived negative impact. Often, when we are tasked to grapple with change, our inclination is to develop a tactical response to perceived problems, when in reality we need to be strategic. For example, a salesperson's tactical approach to a change in a sales cycle might be to improve her cold-call script. The better strategic approach might be to learn about a prospective client's problems and offer tailored solutions.

What's Your Strategic IQ?

What percentage of the time do you spend in strategic mode and what percentage of the time do you spend in tactical? The two numbers should equal 100 percent. Most people need to be more strategic.

What is Tactical?
- Tasks
- Calls
- Activities
- Paper Work

What is Strategic?
- Planning
- Thinking
- Studying

Most People Need to Be More Strategic

So in order to work in solution mode, it is critical to step back and take a strategic approach to virtually everything, including a problem or challenge, and to have balance between "thinking" and "doing." If we truly understand that problems are a matter of perspective, then we can appreciate how solutions-oriented individuals consider problems to merely be temporary setbacks, interim obstacles, or solutions in the making.

> IF YOU CHOOSE TO LIVE IN SOLUTIONS, THE WORLD EAGERLY AWAITS YOUR DREAMS AND PROVIDES EVERY TOOL AND OPPORTUNITY YOU NEED TO TURN THEM INTO REALITY.
> –TONY JEARY

Obstacles, setbacks, and failures simply form a temporary part of life not allowed to become problematic. Almost all problems are solvable, and oftentimes there is a simple solution by just stepping back and looking from a different angle. The more you live in solutions, the more naturally strategic you'll become, and this can have a dramatic impact on your success and, of course, your results.

43.
Ask Questions to Get Leverage

Asking a question creates automatic engagement with another person or an audience of people. You can be much more resourceful, powerful, and productive in life if you learn to ask questions to get specific answers.

Have you ever had a conversation with someone who only answered in two- or three-word sentences, and you walked away feeling like you learned very little or hardly had an encounter at all? They might not have been intentionally giving you short answers. Perhaps you could have phrased your questions better.

A lot of people fail to understand the power of asking good questions. People often move into talking and telling instead of stepping back, asking about priorities, and listening. You'll never know what's on their mind, what's working, what you can help them with, and what's going well in their world if you don't ask.

> **WHEN WE ASK GOOD QUESTIONS WE ARE MORE LIKELY TO GET RESPONSES WORTH LISTENING TO.**

One effective tip for asking stronger questions is to frame your questions in a positive tone. For example, instead of asking, "Hey, what's been going on with you lately?" ask, "Hey, what are the best things going on in your life right now?" Framing things positively assures the direction of the conversation and creates a memory peg with good feelings from the conversation. Just as it is important to ask the right questions of others, it is important to keep yourself at your peak of effectiveness by asking yourself questions like, "What matters most to me?" "What's the best use of my time right now?" "What do I do the best?"

Listening matters. When we ask good questions we are more likely to get responses worth listening to and answers that have valuable information for us personally or professionally. If you want to increase your impact and accomplish even better results, become a master at listening and asking the right questions.

44.
Build Your Future Through Delayed Gratification

You can have anything you want. You just can't have everything at once!

As a high achiever, you're probably chasing a more incredible life, and of course it's within your reach. But chasing too many things at once won't result in success; it will most certainly result in exhaustion and draining your time, energy, and finances. Agree?

> IF ALL OUR EFFORTS WERE REWARDED SHORT-TERM, WE COULD BE MISSING WHAT MATTERS MOST.

Lots of opportunities come your way. Sound right? If you try to tackle them all at once, you could lose your focus and spend 80 hours a week trying to keep up with everything. A lot of business people lose their drive, their health, and then their marriages because they cannot say no. Think about this: Are you spending your health for wealth? I (Tony) did for a while and then I woke up! I don't have to have everything…at least not all right now. Life is a journey, and Peter and I sure do our best today to live it that way.

One smart strategy to achieve what you want without overload—and without taxing your resources—is to stage your successes, purchases, and big spends. Differentiate between your needs versus your wants. You can delay gratification and plan things far into the future and it will mean even more because you planned for it. I can say I want a Rolls Royce, but do I need it now? No. Can I have it in a few years? Sure. Plan things out into the future. Timing is everything.

Remember that you can have anything you want, but give yourself a reality check and consider whether you really need it right now, all at once. Focus on what you really want to have, share, experience, and become. Understand that you can have most anything, so know what you want and have complete clarity about how to bring it into your world so that it compliments—not complicates—your life.

It's tempting to spend all our energy on things that give us immediate payoff, and in business, that's often a good thing. But we should also be focusing our efforts on things that pay off down the road, in both business and in life. If all our efforts were rewarded short-term, we could be missing what matters most.

Have the discipline to wisely delay gratification and build future wins. Consider what you need to spend more time on now to get future rewards. Think about what you should invest in now that will pay off later, relative to your kids, home, financial stability, health, brand, and business. Make a plan, get clear on your goals, and start thinking, organizing, and building for future rewards. Be intentional about doing now what will pay big dividends later.

45.
Leverage Strategic Cascading

Cascading is a tool that everybody is familiar with but most of the time we don't use it as a regular vocabulary word. It's such a powerful concept as a leader to be able to think through when you have a meeting, either internally or externally, on how the information is going to be cascaded down. Sometimes you need to cascade consistent information out to your field, and be able to build tools and then hand them off to your people. This is a way they can be more consistent as they pass things down and the results can be so powerful.

> THE BEST WAY TO ACHIEVE EXTRAORDINARY RESULTS IS TO BECOME INTENTIONAL ABOUT BEING STRATEGIC IN ALL AREAS OF YOUR LIFE.
> –TONY JEARY

As a rule, what we suggest is that at the beginning of the communication, you really think through how that message is going to be cascaded to other people. In a sales scenario for example, if you go to a sales meeting and you or your team is communicating what you have to offer to a potential group of prospects, they need to take that message and cascade it to a board or to another group of people to be able to get a yes. Being able to think about what tools (i.e. a PowerPoint presentation, handout, or video) you can give them to help them be the most influential on your behalf is so valuable.

Strategic Cascading, again, is really a concept or a rule that should be looked at in virtually every single major communication where you have multiple people involved.

46.
Benchmarking for Best Practices

High achievers want to grow and expand as professionals, while also taking their team and organization to higher levels of results. Benchmarking is a powerful way to bring best practices to your organization.

It should be a life-long habit. If you're a high achiever, you should always be on the lookout for the best way to do things, even if it wasn't your idea, and then determine if those ways fit your world.

> **BENCHMARKING IS A POWERFUL WAY TO BRING BEST PRACTICES TO YOUR ORGANIZATION.**

You can benchmark competitors, industry leaders, friends, and mentors. Benchmarking can also come from reading and studying reports, research, and impactful books authored by authorities.

Exploring your industry's best practices and modeling should be part of an implemented system so constant best trends, practices, and technology, are being continually updated. When newest practices and protocols are readily available, top leadership can know more and make better decisions, which leads to more wins in business.

Create a company culture that embraces benchmarking. Look at best practices, model others, and grow your effectiveness.

V. FOCUS

"Lack of direction, not lack of time, is the problem.
We all have twenty-four hour days."
- ZIG ZIGLAR

"Always focus on the front windshield and not the rearview mirror."
- COLIN POWELL

"Obstacles are those frightful things you see
when you take your eyes off your goals."
- HENRY FORD

47.
Understand and Study the Concept of HLAs

There are 168 hours in the week. You spend about 12 hours on personal maintenance and should spend 56 on sleep, which means you're left with about 100 hours. If you think in terms of that limited time block, it makes you really effective at managing time. You want 70–80 percent of your 100-plus hours directed toward your *High Leverage Activities* (HLAs). A good balance is about 35 hours on personal HLAs and about 35 hours on professional HLAs. These are the

> CONTINUALLY ASK YOURSELF, "WHAT'S THE BEST USE OF MY TIME RIGHT NOW?" AND THEN PRIORITIZE ACCORDINGLY.

activities that can give you the most impact in accomplishing your vision, goals, and objectives.

Your High Leverage Activities are those activities that you should be so clear on that you can develop an improved habit of saying no to the things not on your HLA list. You want to learn to say no to what's not mission-critical (distractions) and say yes to those important activities that are focused on helping you reach your goals (see #28). Continually ask yourself, "What's the best use of my time right now?" and then prioritize accordingly.

Again—it works both personally and professionally. We all want to succeed professionally. But of course we desire success in our relationships and families as well. When you have a family focused on the right things (leveraging time), you have a team that will have a profound impact on your success as a family.

Examples of professional HLAs might include:

- Attracting strong, qualified business
- Delivering great value to your clients and colleagues
- Clarifying direction and improving operations
- Building processes, business acumen, best practices, and tools
- Nourishing and building connections, extending value, and positively communicating with them
- Nurturing your people

Some examples of personal HLAs might include:

- Praying
- Investing time with your spouse
- Training or working out
- Learning
- Spending time with your children or grandchildren

Okay, so what are your HLAs? How much of your time do you spend focused on them? How much more could you achieve if you increased that number by 10–20 percent?

Developing the habit of HLA living gives high achievers a strong advantage. It's a habit that successful people often form naturally over time—looking at HLAs and comparing them to other opportunities that flow into their lives. Forming the habit of doing this effectively will serve you in leading your best life.

> NO SINGLE SKILL OR HABIT HAS A MORE POWERFUL IMPACT ON RESULTS THAN THE ABILITY TO ELIMINATE DISTRACTIONS AND FOCUS ON HIGH LEVERAGE ACTIVITIES (HLAs).
> –TONY JEARY

48.
Focus—The Opposite of Distraction

Often, the difference between someone successful and someone who isn't is extreme focus, because what you invest in is what will grow. You really do get more of what you focus on. If you focus on your relationship, you'll have a good one. If you invest in your business, you'll have a good one. Invest time, resources, and energy in your business, marriage, and kids, and those things will grow.

SUCCESSFUL ENTREPRENEURS MUST HAVE EXTREME FOCUS.

In today's ultra-competitive world, getting superior results faster is critical to success - and so many people want it! However, this hectic speed of life makes it easy to become sidetracked by things that steal priority and make us less effective. Before long you've lost focus and don't even know it until your business or a relationship begins to suffer.

We've seen many entrepreneurs operate in "overwhelmed" mode. They become mired in the daily activities, unable to get off the hamster wheel of meetings and reactionary emails, calls, and activities, and then they lose focus. The business goals begin to drift farther and farther away.

Successful entrepreneurs must have extreme focus. It's easy to get pulled away from our goals by people, places, ideas, or things. Every material thing you own requires time and energy. Every new purchase, every idea, and every new person who enters your office or day requires attention. It takes an intentionally focused person to minimize distractions. And focus is the opposite of distraction and is critical to high achievers.

The first three chapters in Tony's book, *Strategic Acceleration*, describe the importance of developing clarity about your vision, as well as understanding the "why" behind it. A clear and authentic vision enables willing changes in behavior and sets you up for success. Gaining clarity on your vision, however, is just the first step in the *Strategic Acceleration* process. The second step—focus—will teach you how to better develop this important skill.

> FOCUS IS A THINKING SKILL ACQUIRED AS A RESULT OF MENTAL DISCIPLINE.
>
> –TONY JEARY

I (Peter) have all kinds of tricks to get myself focused and diffuse distractions. Once when I was facing several severe difficult business challenges simultaneously, I went out and purchased a GI Camouflage Helmet and presented it to my lawyer. I told him we would be going to war and I needed him to be thinking 24/7 of ways to win the war. Losing the war was not acceptable by any standard. He placed the helmet in his office in a very prominent place. I wanted him to be thinking of solving my problems all the time. It worked! We won the war.

If you ever find yourself in need of setting short-term objectives, get a physical item as a visual image to keep your team focused, so they never forget how important their support is to you. The reason there are winners and losers is because usually the losers lose their focus and are not totally and completely absorbed with the success of the objectives.

Once you have the ability to focus on your vision (and all of the strategies, tactics, and actions required for its success), you will be ready for the final step—execution—and you will act on and accomplish your vision results faster.

49.
Aim for 87 Percent

There's a saying that goes, "Excellence adds value; perfection just adds time." So many people are out for perfection to such a degree that they either stop because they can never reach their desired state, or they put in significantly more time than there is value for the last few percent.

I (Peter) have a concept I call the Rule of 87 Percent. You will be amazed at the results if you quit being a perfectionist and understand that as a rule, 87 percent is just fine. Do you want to be known for value? Do you want

> DON'T ALLOW YOUR STANDARDS AND COMMITMENT TO MASTERY TO INTERFERE WITH GETTING THINGS DONE; 87% IS OFTEN GOOD ENOUGH. BE OKAY WITH IT SOMETIMES AND MOVE ON. –PETER THOMAS

to be known for excellence? Absolutely. Oftentimes, excellence comes in at 87 percent. Striving for perfection will sidetrack your results and make your customers wait. They want results, and they want them fast.

When you're negotiating a deal or engaging in any kind of business proposition, don't lose sight of what's important. Focus on production and the critical factors in the project. Focus on your highest-leveraged items and activities and when you hit 87 percent success, celebrate!

Why not 100 percent? Because in all our years of experience in coaching and living in the entrepreneurial world, we've seen analysis paralysis and the stress of focusing on perfection cause people to lose more than they win. If you're continually focused on achieving 100 percent, you'll be continually disappointed, especially where other people are involved.

IF YOU'RE CONTINUALLY
FOCUSED ON ACHIEVING
100 PERCENT, YOU'LL
BE CONTINUALLY
DISAPPOINTED,
ESPECIALLY WHERE OTHER
PEOPLE ARE INVOLVED.

High expectations are great, but there are always other factors in any situation. In most cases, 87 percent will be just as good as 100 or better because of the worrying, stress, and negative energy that come with trying to achieve a perfect score.

50.
Maintain Your Personal Agenda in Hard Times

No matter what comes your way, remember to stay focused on your personal agenda, values, and goals. Some entrepreneurs forget this, and when they hit a roadblock or obstacle, it disrupts everything they had planned and impacts the way they think about themselves, their business, and others. But you simply cannot cave when things go wrong. You need to maintain your personal agenda, keep pushing through it, and stay the course (see #21).

> **THERE ARE ALWAYS DISTRACTIONS THAT THREATEN THE ACCOMPLISHMENTS YOU WANT TO MAKE, SO KEEP YOUR EYES STRAIGHT AHEAD.**

Life is a series of peaks and valleys, and obstacles are inevitable. What many people overlook is that episodes of turmoil are excellent times to set some new personal objectives. Build an environment that motivates you and it will help you through those rough patches. But also realize that God made the world and it's not perfect. There are billions of people in it and sometimes they can impact you negatively.

How do you cope? How will you remain focused on your goals and relationships? One way is to deflect any drama and minimize it when you can. I (Tony) can recall a time when one of my employees called because her car broke down, as it had several times in the past. I helped her and it ate up valuable time. It also became a pattern. The next time it occurred, I didn't engage in the drama or attempt to solve her problem.

I encouraged her to solve it. My personal agenda on that particular day was to keep moving forward and create results tied to my list of priorities for the day (especially my MITs: Most Important Things), so I didn't let her problem, or the fact that she may or may not show up, ruin my day.

> DISTRACTIONS WASTE OUR TIME. SAYING NO TO THE THINGS THAT DON'T MATTER PAYS OFF BIG. REMEMBER, FOCUS IS THE OPPOSITE OF DISTRACTION.
> —TONY JEARY

If you take on everyone's problems, they can become your problems. They can negatively impact your mind, thinking, and clients, and can be a huge drain on your energy and resources. There are always distractions that threaten the accomplishments you want to make, so keep your eyes straight ahead. Think about your personal agenda each day, and move toward your goals with laser focus.

51.
Appreciate (and Invest Time in) What You Want More of

If you want to grow your portfolio, you'll have to invest. This basic rule applies to all areas in life.

Appreciate what you want more of in other areas of your life, not just finances. Invest in the lives of loved ones to solidify your relationships. There are six basic elements common to all human existence, and how we combine them provides the evidence of our life management. This concept is also known by many as the "Balance Wheel of Life," and it embraces the principle that the more balanced we are in each of the six areas, the smoother our wheel of life will roll. We say it's not really about focusing on perfect balance; it's about managed balance. For example, when you're in your early twenties, you often want to be out of balance and be heavy on education, or if you have someone in your family who needs extra

WHEN YOU VERBALLY APPRECIATE SOMETHING SPECIFIC, PEOPLE WANT TO DO MORE OF IT. IT'S THAT SIMPLE.

care because of health, you want to invest extra time with and supporting them.

This concept moves all the way down to even what you say or write on any given day. I (Tony) send texts to my girls almost daily, appreciating them for making good decisions and they have become incredible young adults who make exceptional decisions. And I continue to appreciate this with the focused thinking of wanting more and more positive daily decisions from my kids. When you verbally appreciate something specific, people want to do more of it. It's that simple.

> KNOW WHAT REALLY, REALLY MAKES YOU HAPPY, THEN BUILD A LIFE AROUND IT.
> –TONY JEARY

Our families are one of God's greatest gifts. We are charged with the responsibility of nurturing family relationships, with the overall goal of creating happy, secure, and successful families. The common threads of faithfulness and commitment hold successful families together, for those attributes create an atmosphere of love and trust in which families can thrive. If you want a great family, invest in them and appreciate them - a lot! Likewise, if you want a healthy company or a healthy body, invest in them and the results will multiply.

VI. BRAND

"In this ever-changing society, the most powerful and enduring brands are built from the heart. They are real and sustainable. Their foundations are stronger because they are built with the strength of the human spirit, not an ad campaign.
The companies that are lasting are those that are authentic."
- HOWARD SCHULTZ

"Branding is about everything."
- TOM PETERS

"Think of yourself as a brand. You need to be remembered. What will they remember you for? What defines you? If you have it in you, do something that defines you. Invent something, develop a unique skill, get noticed for something—it creates a talking point."
- CHRIS ARNOLD

52.
Be Known for Something

What are you known for? You don't have to be good at everything, but you should be excellent in at least one area. Find that one thing and be the expert. Know your God-given talents.

I (Tony) get results. My clients and prospects know that I help them get what they want faster, and that I am a true "encourager." I (Peter) am a deal maker, and I've been very successful at it. I had a vision for making Century 21 Canada a success when no one else believed in it, and I did. I sold the company for many millions.

> YOU REALLY DO GET MORE OF WHAT YOU FOCUS ON—FOCUS ON THINGS THAT SUPPORT YOUR GOALS AND VISION.
> –TONY JEARY

Whatever you are good at, be known for it, and consistently excel in that field. Understand what's driving that success and identify any areas that are holding you back.

If you don't feel like you're good at any one particular thing, ask yourself why. You may already be very successful. On the other hand, you may have struggled with achievement and may not be as successful as you would like. Whichever the case, it may be a good idea to look at the choices you have made and the principles governing those choices. Regardless of your current achievement level, you can always improve. Get clear on your strengths; know yourself well. Leverage your strengths and talents.

53.
Brand Yourself

A successful brand (reputation) reflects who you are. Your brand is your unique promise. Build a brand based on not only who you want to be and how you want to live, but who you actually are and the core of how you live today.

> **BUILD A BRAND BASED ON NOT ONLY WHO YOU WANT TO BE AND HOW YOU WANT TO LIVE, BUT WHO YOU ACTUALLY ARE.**

What's important to your prospective client? Chances are, it isn't just about making money. People want to do business with people they trust. People also want to do business with people they respect. They want to know that you can get the job done, but they also have specific values that are important to them such as security, follow-up communication, and relationship. Understand what's important to people and what they value, and build your brand authentically. Be who you say you are.

As an entrepreneur, what is it that makes you stand out from everyone else? If you're a realtor for instance, what separates you from the rest of the pack? Are you a luxury home seller? Or do you focus on a specific neighborhood? Brand yourself distinctly and create a profile that people remember. Marketing your brand to your clients can be just as important as business processes, communication, technology, and sales.

No matter what your brand is, make sure you're known as someone who follows through. It doesn't matter what business ventures we've entered over the years, there have always been people with integrity and people without it. The ones without integrity are the ones that no one

#	Element	Description	Name:		Date:
1.	Brand Description	What is the essence of my brand positioning? (10 word phrase summarizing from the 20 items below)			
2.	Core Value Proposition	Core characteristics that are valuable to my effectiveness			
3.	Business Priorities	Parameters and priorities for how I operate on a daily basis (what matters most)			
4.	_____ is	Characteristics that describe me			
5.	_____ is Not	Characteristics that do not describe me			
6.	Uniqueness	What truly makes me unique? What distinctions separate me in my niche?			
7.	Packaging	The tools, expertise, image, etc. to be leveraged to the market			
8.	Visual Image	Physical image/appearance			
9.	Mission Stmt.	What drives my decisions?			
10.	Brand Power	The "thrust" behind my reputation			
11.	Tagline	Benefit-driven, descriptive (what I say often)			
12.	Positioning	Role(s) within the market/organization			
13.	Business Motto	Statement of approach to business life			
14.	What People Think Of You	My perception of how I am perceived			
15.	What People Are Missing	My beliefs on what others are misunderstanding about me			
16.	Attributes Prized in the Workplace	What attributes do I possess that the market (my organization) values?			
17.	Passions	What things am I passionate about?			
18.	Top Communication Opportunities	Top meetings/presentations where my brand is impacted			
19.	Where Is My Audience/ Prospect?	Who are those I most want to impact?			
20.	External Barriers	Real world roadblocks			
21.	Internal Barriers	Self-imposed roadblocks			

PERSONAL BRANDING MATRIX™

wants to do business with, and that is consistent across industries. In the Bible, Isaiah 32:8 reads, "But the noble man devises noble plans; and by noble plans he stands" (NASB). Be noble. Be the one people trust.

Loyalty, trust, and nobility go a long way toward making your business grow. Think of it this way: When you are in an important business presentation against your competitor, if you don't know your prospect and they don't know you, it all comes down to who they feel they can trust. People make gut decisions based on who they like and trust. Can they trust you?

A lot of it comes down to the way you have built and communicated

> WE ALL HAVE A BRAND (A REPUTATION). TOP LEADERS ARE STRATEGIC ABOUT THEIRS. THEY THINK ABOUT AND WRITE DOWN WHO THEY WANT TO BECOME.
> —TONY JEARY

your brand. People want to be confident that they're not going to be misled or stabbed in the back. They need to know they're spending their money wisely and investing in good people. Build your brand on nobility—it's not just about marketing your achievements.

54.
Develop a Memorable, Influential Persona

Are you memorable? What specifically do you want people to remember about you? It's not just your brand, or your personality—your trademark expression, style, or persona also make you memorable . . . or not.

Have you ever met someone you just knew was different than everyone else? Maybe they were humorous, carefree, or extremely positive when everyone else around you wasn't, and you remembered them for that. That's how you want others to remember you.

Entrepreneurs are different; they don't necessarily fit into a corporate setting. Their persona and personality don't fit into 9-to-5 jobs. Entrepreneurs value freedom, creativity, and the power to choose, and that makes them different from the majority. Think of the big personalities with memorable personas, such as Richard Branson, or Donald Trump, or Herb Kelleher. Other leaders aren't as significant or don't stand out, even if they've achieved a lot. But you don't have to have the most dynamic personality to be memorable.

> YOU DON'T HAVE TO HAVE THE MOST DYNAMIC PERSONALITY TO BE MEMORABLE.

One aspect of being memorable is how well you make an impact in someone else's life. People remember those who impact their lives. Since most people's favorite subject is themselves, one way to make an immediate impact is to ask them about their life. No one likes to be ignored. Yet we live in a society where everyone is ignoring everyone else in favor of texting, emailing, and talking about themselves. You could be different and memorable by being focused on other people. Say, "Tell me more!" Be genuinely interested in their response.

This is an area that you could probably improve in. Most of us can. So ask yourself, "Am I genuinely interested in people, to the point that I am building a positive, strategic presence that significantly affects my results?" If this is an area that needs work, start asking questions and being genuinely interested in others.

55.
Be Real. People Appreciate Transparency!

This rule isn't just about honesty with others; it's about being honest and true to yourself. Are you really living the life you want to live? If you're not, it can show. So stop for a moment—right now—to think about your life, and about what you really want. What are you doing that you don't like to do? Who are you working with that you shouldn't be investing in? As a leader, it's critically important that you're honest with yourself. You can only pretend to be happy for so long.

If you're living someone else's dream and not your own, it will show. You can be short, angry, unhappy, and impatient with colleagues and friends. Your clients can often see that you aren't enthusiastic about your own life and business. Enthusiasm is contagious and so is negativity and dissatisfaction. You can feel it when someone does not authentically like what they do. You can see it when the waitress, flight attendant, or executive is unhappy with their job, and it's a negative reflection on the business.

> IF YOU'RE LIVING SOMEONE ELSE'S DREAM AND NOT YOUR OWN, IT WILL SHOW.

Oftentimes entrepreneurs want speed, so they get caught up in things they don't love or things out of their capability. But in order to be happy, successful, and authentic it's best to know what you want and to live it. When you're honest with yourself you can be honest with your clients. We're all imperfect at doing life, and being real matters. When the people you work with know your heart, they will realize that delivering value and being real are more important than being perfect.

In talking with a mutual friend of ours, Jay Rodgers, a highly success-ful entrepreneur, he said, "Always play with your cards face up." What does that mean? It means that you might as well be open and honest about what you want to achieve, which is different from the old days of being cunning. When you're open and transparent, you have the free-dom you need to advance further and faster. Do what you love and love what you do. Your associates and clients will thank you for it.

56.
Your Body Language and Appearance Impact Your Success

Most high achievers understand that it's important to be presentable. After all, you are your business and when prospects meet you, they'll judge you and your success, and their potential to have success, by the things they see. It doesn't matter if it's your car, your office, or your clothes. People will form an opinion of you by what they see.

But looking good isn't just about how others perceive you. Some may argue that it's not important what you look like, because it's what's inside that counts. In the past decade, there's been a big trend toward casual work environments and being sloppy, wrinkled, and comfortable, especially in the tech space. In companies that are trying to attract a younger mindset, the cultural dress code might be a radically dressed-down environment. But if you're an entrepreneur, keep in mind not only your employees' perceptions and desires, but your customers'. What kind of business are you trying to attract? And how do you personally feel when you dress for success?

> WHEN PROSPECTS MEET YOU, THEY'LL JUDGE YOU AND YOUR SUCCESS, AND THEIR POTENTIAL TO HAVE SUCCESS, BY THE THINGS THEY SEE.

It's about strategic presence. I (Tony) devoted a whole chapter on this in my book *Strategic Acceleration*. What do people see when they see you? Do you smile? Or do you exude a stressful energy, always looking down at your mobile device while texting? People will often judge you based on their first thirty seconds of an encounter. That leaves no room for error.

Part of building your brand is the way you look. This is beyond vanity; it's about excellence. Each day you make choices: Do I want to be excellent today? Do I want to think, communicate, and convey a strong, authentic, and positive image? You will be judged on the way you look, think, and communicate. A smile makes people perceive you as approachable. A scowl, or ignoring people while you text, sends a different message. Truth is, most people build a reputation based on who they are, what they've done, or how they look, but they aren't intentional about it.

> BE STRATEGIC ABOUT YOUR BRAND AND REPUTATION; DON'T JUST LET IT HAPPEN.
> –TONY JEARY

Every day we are being pre-judged by the way we look, act, talk, and dress. Judging is the only way to assess a situation, a deal, or the players involved. Judging is simply using our eyes, ears, and senses to determine what we think or believe about someone else. Are you doing your best to convey the best impression? Be wardrobe appropriate, use open body language, and send the message that you are successful and confident.

57.
Do Favors in Advance (FIA)

Remember the last time someone did something nice and unexpected for you? Maybe they sent you a gift, referred you to a new client, or perhaps they performed a task to help you out so that you didn't have to do it. Favors in advance are favors that you do for people regardless of your status with them, or desired outcome. Instead of doing favors because you expect something in return, develop an attitude of paying it forward and giving value in advance.

> **INSTEAD OF DOING FAVORS BECAUSE YOU EXPECT SOMETHING IN RETURN, DEVELOP AN ATTITUDE OF PAYING IT FORWARD AND GIVING VALUE IN ADVANCE.**

We have seen numerous people over the years who are hesitant to do for others, unless that individual is going to pay off in business or do something for them. But that thinking is just wrong. Do things to help others. Think of the people who are in your inner circle in business, and continually do favors for them. Will you extend your database and share your connections? Live in abundance versus scarcity.

This rule works for strangers as well as clients, friends, and prospects. People like to do business with people who do things for them and who work to build a platform of trust. Why not be a giver?

We both like to give things away. Whether it's a book, a LifePilot binder, or something else that can enhance another person's life, we've found it helpful to have tools on hand to give to others. Tony has them in the trunk of his car and carries resources in his briefcase for chance meetings. Have a bookshelf of giveaways. It's about being prepared with an arsenal of information so you can do favors in advance. Help people win, and be generous.

58.
Be a "Connector"

Being a person who connects the dots is valuable and powerful, because they make things happen. Being a connector is a way to bring unforeseen value to other people as well as to yourself. It's really natural for some, and others need to put thinking power to this rule. It is about influence. And every entrepreneur and leader needs the leverage and knowledge that others provide. No one can do it alone.

Continually expand your network because you will need the help of others to accelerate your achievement. Create your own "connection database" and build on it. The key to building a solid database is a primary mindset that involves being aware of others who may be able to work with you in the future in some capacity.

LOOK FOR WAYS TO CREATE WINS BY CONNECTING PEOPLE WITH OTHERS WHO HAVE THE KNOWLEDGE AND EXPERTISE TO HELP THEM GET THE RESULTS THEY WANT.

The first step in identifying people to add to your database is to meet a lot of people and learn as much about them as possible. This involves really listening to what others have to say and asking a lot of questions - blindly collecting business cards does not count. Even though this may be awkward for some, overcoming any hesitancy to meet and visit with strangers is a part of the mindset we suggest be developed.

Some of our best connections have happened unexpectedly, where we met someone who turned out to be important to a deal. Be open to meeting people on vacations, in business, or wherever you are. Look for ways to create wins by connecting people with others who have the knowledge and expertise to help them get the results they want. Build and nurture your database of connections so that people are always happy to hear from you.

If you like people, you can connect them. They win and you win. I (Tony) have 25,000 people in my contact database, and I use these connections to help my clients connect and grow. Do you have a system for your business cards and connections to create a database? What does that system look like?

LIFE IS A SERIES OF PRESENTATIONS . . . MAKE EACH ONE COUNT.

–TONY JEARY

Get the contact, program it into your phone or database, and develop a system. Once you do, nurture your contacts. Entrepreneurs that are connectors nourish people and give them notes, cards, and gifts of value. It doesn't have to be a large gift, either. It can be a book, an article, video, card, or just a suggested URL.

Think of ways you can nurture your contacts and build your list! Connect others where it makes mutual sense for them, and you create automatic wins for yourself.

59.
Be Interested, Not Just Interesting

How many boring sales presentations have you sat through where the presenter drones on and on about their product or service? Meanwhile, around the conference table, people are falling asleep, checking their text messages, or surfing the Internet. The salesperson keeps going, seemingly oblivious to what's going on in the room around him. That's the trait of a poor salesperson, and we've all seen this happen.

> **BE GENUINELY INTERESTED IN WHAT OTHERS HAVE TO SAY.**

As a leader, it is particularly important that when you research a company or a business opportunity, make sure you also understand the humans within the culture. When you talk to them or meet with them face-to-face, don't let your previous assumptions or knowledge about the company override the human factor. Listen to them talk to understand their personalities and ask questions when the time is right, with the right words, the right strategy, and the appropriate mindset. People ultimately will make the decision on whether or not to buy your product or service, or to do business with you. This is why it's essential to be a good people person.

Be genuinely interested in what others have to say. Listening will help you ensure you're on track with your presentation or communication, or if you need to make a shift. Remember, it's not about you—it's about them.

60.
Ensure Strategic Alignment Between Your Branding, Marketing, and Sales

In many companies, what you have are silos of individuals in each of the different areas of branding, marketing, and sales. In fact, sometimes you even have different department heads and they aren't always working in unison like they could. If this happens, step back and make sure you are really clear on the branding message that you want to be communicating.

From a marketing perspective, all of the marketing tools in your arsenal should be congruent with your branding message so that you have the power, that sameness, if you will—the same colors, the same thinking, the same words, and the same methodology. Think about your web presence, videos, brochures, PowerPoints, handouts, and leave-behinds. Having that alignment can bring business in and make sales a slam-dunk. (In the Appendix is a marketing tool audit to help you really look at your marketing efforts/tools in an efficient way.)

We've seen it many times where people in the sales arena are pulling from the marketing arsenal, and it's not always consistent with the brand. That alignment can be a huge deal. Make a commitment today that in every organization you start, run, manage, or lead, you will ensure all three of these important areas are strategically aligned.

> ALL OF THE MARKETING TOOLS IN YOUR MARKETING ARSENAL SHOULD BE CONGRUENT WITH YOUR BRANDING MESSAGE.

61.
Be Presentation Ready

As an entrepreneur, there are always people investing in you, and there are almost always strategic partnership opportunities. Being presentation ready for each one of those stakeholders can often make or break an opportunity.

You should continuously be presentation ready, so when the phone call comes in from an investor, you're ready to give them a brief; if you meet someone at an event, you're ready to recruit them; or if an unexpected meeting comes up, you can pull from your arsenal.

> *LIFE IS A SERIES OF PRESENTATIONS,* **AND BEING READY FOR EACH OPPORTUNITY IS A GREAT ASSET TO HAVE IN YOUR CORNER.**

A person's *Presentation Universe* is pretty large and expands well beyond just the "big presentations." Life is a series of presentations, and being ready for each opportunity is a great asset to have in your corner. Do an inventory of all the potential types of presentations you may need to give: a 30-second elevator speech, a two-minute conversation, a formal presentation, a staff meeting, and talks for recruiting and investors. Outline some key points for each of these talks and practice them. The more ready you are in advance for each of these opportunities, the more likely you'll walk away with your desired outcome.

VII. LEADERSHIP

*"As we look ahead into the next century,
leaders will be those who empower others."*
– BILL GATES

*"The greatest leader is not necessarily
the one who does the greatest things.
He is the one that gets the people to do the greatest things."*
- RONALD REAGAN

"To handle yourself, use your head; to handle others, use your heart."
- ELEANOR ROOSEVELT

62.
Freedom Comes from Absolute Discipline

This one is worth repeating: Freedom comes from absolute discipline. Is there a relationship between freedom and discipline? We say yes! In fact, the great Aristotle said it first: "Through discipline comes freedom."

When you think of the word freedom, the word discipline is probably not the first thought that comes to mind. In fact, it seems like an oxymoron. Most people equate freedom to having fewer rules and being more spontaneous.

Freedom doesn't mean having no direction, responsibilities, or limitations. It is about choices and decisions you make for your life and having the discipline to do the things that support the life you really want to lead.

> **THE MORE DISCIPLINED YOU ARE IN STAYING ON TRACK AND EXECUTING THINGS THAT SUPPORT YOUR PROFESSIONAL GOALS, THE MORE FREEDOM YOU WILL HAVE TO SUPPORT YOUR PERSONAL GOALS.**

A part of being disciplined and gaining freedom means once you decide which things mean the most to you, you learn to say no to things that don't support your goals (see #28). Most people say yes to things far too often that end up having no value to them and take up time that could either be spent pursuing goals or could be used for downtime or family time. It's not only okay to say no but it is crucial to keeping focused on the things that matter most, and that will give you the freedom you desire.

What freedoms do you currently wish you had that you don't? What disciplines can you establish that will help you gain those freedoms? The more disciplined you are in staying on track and executing things that support your professional goals, the more freedom you will have to support your personal goals. You will gain time, freedom, and energy, and you will continually be able to renew and refresh yourself.

> YOUR MOST IMPORTANT POWER IS YOUR POWER TO CHOOSE—YOUR CHOICES DETERMINE YOUR LIFE.
> –PETER THOMAS

63.
Develop Perseverance

One of the traits of high achievers is the ability to keep going, over and over again, no matter what obstacles they face.

Forbes magazine published a study in September 2013 on "The Six Disciplines Entrepreneurs Need to Succeed." One of those six disciplines was mental toughness. If you're resilient, you will be able to bounce back from the setbacks you will face. Some will be small, and some will be so big that they seem overwhelming. You must cultivate mental toughness and the determination to press on despite obstacles if you're going to survive and thrive in the business world.

Simply being willing to keep going, switch gears, attempt new things, and work harder than others are willing to work will win in the end. Having an attitude of perseverance will keep you focused on the end goal and keep you solution-oriented.

> NOTHING PERSUADES MORE EFFECTIVELY THAN A LEADER WHO SETS THE RIGHT EXAMPLE FOR HIS TEAM, CHILDREN, ASSOCIATES, AND COLLEAGUES TO FOLLOW.
> –TONY JEARY

We both have had major setbacks in life. I (Tony) became a millionaire before I was thirty, then lost everything. I (Peter) lost my son suddenly. But we both bounced back by having an attitude of perseverance and determining to make something positive out of our traumatic experiences.

John Quincy Adams once said, "Patience and perseverance have a

> ## DEVELOP PERSEVERANCE AND YOU'LL BE ABLE TO BREAK THROUGH ANY SETBACKS THAT COME YOUR WAY.

magical effect before which difficulties disappear and obstacles vanish." Develop perseverance and you'll be able to break through any setbacks that come your way.

64.
Live by Documented Personal Standards

If you've ever worked for a large company, you probably know what corporate standards are, and how a standard transmits to the culture. Cultures are built on the standards of the organization and some leaders go to great lengths to create cultures that reflect their personal standards.

We both have specific personal defined standards. These are more than just beliefs; they're values and standards that we live by. I (Tony) have twelve specific standards and I know them well, but I also have them written down. They include daily prayer; meeting my teams' inspirational needs each day; looking at my client pipeline; studying my daily to-do list; eating, exercising, and living healthy; and doing favors in advance for people. Peter's include having gratitude each day, telling his wife and friends "I love you," exercising, and making healthy choices.

> **IF YOU HAVE A PERSONAL STANDARD CENTERED AROUND ACCELERATING YOUR RESULTS, YOU'LL PERFORM TASKS WITH ACCELERATED TIME FRAMES ASSOCIATED WITH THEM.**

Be aware of what standards you want to incorporate into your daily life. Think of what they are, write them down, and reassess them. Standards on speed, for instance, are generally very low. Today we have technology that equips us to do more, and in a quicker time frame. You no longer have to wait until Monday at the office to review a document, for instance. If you have a personal standard centered around accelerating your results, you'll perform tasks with accelerated time frames associated with them.

The person with the highest standards is the person who lives in mastery (see #41). If you don't want to have high standards, be average. Some people are okay with average, mediocre results. But you're probably reading this because you want more than that, so develop personal standards that you and everyone around you can live by.

65.
Channel Your Emotions and Control Your Ego

There are external factors to your success and there are internal factors. Living a well-managed life includes managing your emotions and all of the inner workings of your mind. How well do you manage your emotions?

No one knows yourself better than you, so prepare and plan for managing the myriad of emotions that will come as you face the challenging yet exciting life of an entrepreneur. In life and relationships, emotions and ego are always a factor. How well you control those things will impact your ability to connect with others and persuade them to see things the way that you need them to in order to achieve results.

> LEARNING TO SEPARATE EMOTION FROM BUSINESS DECISIONS WILL HELP YOU ACCELERATE YOUR RESULTS.

Sometimes we don't see that our own emotions are creating destructive results. It could be anger, stress, or ego that's getting in the way of bonding with colleagues, attracting new clients, or closing deals. Emotions can impact a relationship in both positive and negative ways. Similarly, people often make business decisions (or don't make them) based on emotion.

> LEADERSHIP IS SIMPLY A RESULTS CONTEST.
>
> –TONY JEARY

Learning to separate emotion from business decisions will help you accelerate your results.

66.
Be a Person of Influence

When you have a positive impact on people, places, and things, and create momentum and results, you have influence. When others know you as a person of action, and rely on you to think alongside them, they trust that you have intellect, vision, and the ability to make things happen. Influence is comprised of respect and confidence.

Influencers make things happen. It's a trait that most powerful people possess, no matter what personality style they have. Influence is the one thing that matters in business, above all else. Influencers have the ability to change other people's decisions, get people to buy, and convince others to see their point of view. People with influence have already built up an arsenal of respect, trust, credibility, and brand strength. People want to be around them. Clients, colleagues, and prospects want to be a part of their world.

> THE DIFFERENCE BETWEEN THOSE WHO LEAD SUCCESSFUL LIVES AND THOSE WHO DON'T IS THAT THOSE WHO ARE SUCCESSFUL TRANSLATE THEIR IDEAS INTO ACTION.
>
> —PETER THOMAS

When we were putting this book together, we talked about the "it" factor that some people seem to have. Celebrities have it, and that's what makes them unique and able to captivate an audience. Some entrepreneurs have it, too. We could debate whether the "it" factor is simply something you're born with, because charisma and the ability to charm and captivate others might just be intrinsic and not learned. However, whether you have "it" or not, you certainly can learn to be a person of influence. Influence

151

goes hand-in-hand with the "it" factor.

Customers are naturally drawn to an influential brand and a person of influence. This is one of the best things you could ever do for your life or business because when you develop the trait of influence, people, deals, and money will gravitate toward you, as you influence and organize them to success.

INFLUENCE IS THE ONE THING THAT MATTERS IN BUSINESS, ABOVE ALL ELSE.

The ability to make it happen is a key trait of successful individuals. If you are committed to mastery, make this a strategic activity. Dedicate yourself to becoming a person of influence.

67.
Delegate a Lot More

The magic of delegating is getting things done faster, period! When you delegate smartly, you're often creating space for the High Leverage Activities (HLAs), those things that matter the most (see #47).

A good sign that you need to delegate more is if you are continually tired, overstressed, overworked, and unhealthy. If you don't have time to work out or if you're constantly rushing from one place to another, chances are you need to delegate more small things to make space for the big things. Think intelligently about your life and manage time more wisely. It's the foundation to reaching a higher level.

The best way to look at delegation is to examine your goals and activities and identify which things absolutely cannot be delegated. Lunch with a client, for instance, is something that perhaps only you can do. However, sending an email to a prospect might be something that your sales person or assistant could do instead. Building relationships shouldn't be delegated, but administrative tasks are a perfect example of things that can be delegated effectively.

Once you start strategically delegating, it can become addictive and you'll want to delegate more because it will give you more time and energy to focus on the things that you enjoy and are good at doing. Be careful not to micromanage once you delegate and negate the process. Your relation-

> AN ESSENTIAL FUNCTION OF LEADERSHIP IS TO PERSUADE AND MOTIVATE OTHERS TO PURSUE EXCELLENCE BY HELPING THEM BECOME WILLING TO EXCEED EXPECTATIONS.
>
> –TONY JEARY

ships can become stronger and your business offers will often increase as a result. Your effectiveness as a leader—in fact, your whole world—can change.

68.
Utilize Personality Profiling

The most successful people in the world know that there are many different types of personalities, and selling to them, building relationships, and working with many different people requires finesse and understanding. Not everyone is like you. In fact, most people aren't. So how do you best relate to the world around you?

> **UNDERSTANDING PERSONALITY STYLES WILL HELP YOU EXCEL AT BUSINESS.**

Most people filter life through their own eyes. It is natural to see others the way you think. But what if someone thinks completely differently and you don't know it? Understanding personality styles will help you excel at business. If you're into details, and someone else isn't, you might be in a meeting and go on and on in a presentation, with the prospective buyer who only desires a high-level, fast overview. Your many details might make them angry or hesitant. But if you'd known that the prospective buyer wasn't a detail person, you could have adapted your presentation to give a high-level view.

In our office, we use the DISC personality profile to determine a client's personality. Below are some key points based on the DISC personality profile:

- A "D" personality is a driver, a personality that wants results. If you bore a D with details, you are certain to lose. D personalities will make buying decisions based on results and speed. If they determine you to be a slow, detailed, methodical thinker, it might work against you. But if you perceive those traits as an asset, you'll miss the mark when it comes to communicating with your target.

- An "I" personality is an influencer, a personality that likes to build relationships. They like to be social and participate in events where there is an opportunity to be people-centered. Often an I is persuasive and warm, building great alliances. They want people to support their ideas and opinions and get to know them. They want to be recognized.
- An "S" personality is steady and nurturing. They care about taking care of others and being very service-oriented. They want to talk feelings, not facts—they want approval. They don't like to be backed into a corner.
- A "C" personality is very compliant. They are analytical problem-solvers and detail-oriented. They like to perfect processes and work plans. Their high expectations of themselves and others can at times be critical. They want you to be sensitive of their time, and they want details. The more systematic and logical, the better for them.

Understand personality profiling. Learn how to incorporate it into your life. (See Dr. Rohm's site at www.personalityinsights.com.) Now this of course also applies to your personal life and helps tremendously with your spouse and kids, as well as professionally with bosses, employees, co-workers, and clients. If you don't take the time to learn the language everyone else is speaking, you'll lose. Don't be blind to the fact that you must learn the variances in personality profiles.

69.
Support a High-Energy Culture

As high achievers in leadership roles, we sometimes sense that things could and should be done faster, but our organizational culture operates with reduced expectations and accepts less-than-superior results. The culture, in this case, would be defined as "low energy" when in fact, it is "high energy" that gets things done, and gets them done well.

A High-Energy Culture has some unique characteristics. Does your team have these traits?

- Clarity: The creation of a High-Energy Culture begins with driving the clarity of purpose down through the organization so that every member understands the vision, direction, and goals.
- Focus: Every member of the culture knows what is expected but also understands their role in the organizational vision.
- Action-oriented: A High-Energy Culture does not procrastinate; it sheds bureaucracy and is focused on getting things done.

> THE ENERGY LEVEL OF THE CULTURE AROUND YOU IS A DIRECT RESULT OF THE CORE BELIEFS SHARED BY EVERYONE INVOLVED.

- Solutions-driven: A High-Energy Culture is solutions-driven rather than problems-focused.
- Opportunity: A High-Energy Culture continually seeks and recognizes new opportunities that will help it win.
- Winning: A High-Energy Culture is focused on winning, and it is

the habit of winning that continues to fuel the high-energy level of the enterprise.

> HIGH ACHIEVERS SET UP SYSTEMS, PEOPLE, AND PROCESSES TO HELP THEM DISCOVER AND SEE DISTINCTIONS AND ACHIEVE GREATER RESULTS.
> –TONY JEARY

The energy level of the culture around you is a direct result of the core beliefs shared by everyone involved. It has a huge impact on what level of achievement will become reality. An average energy level may be able to produce good, satisfactory results. An above-average energy level may produce above-average to superior results. Seek to create a High-Energy Culture to produce masterful results, faster.

VIII. PEOPLE

"Failure defeats losers, failure inspires winners."
– ROBERT T. KIYOSAKI

"The first time someone shows you who they are, believe them."
- MAYA ANGELOU

*"Don't be afraid of enemies who attack you.
Be afraid of the friends who flatter you."*
- DALE CARNEGIE

70.
Surround Yourself with Successful, Positive People!

We all have a choice with whom we spend time. And with all the billions of people on this planet, life is simply too short not to spend your valuable time with inspiring ones. Gravitate toward the people who make you happy and who support and motivate you, and gravitate away from people who are negative, uninspiring, angry, or self-defeating. And that, of course, includes whom you hire. Are you surrounded by dream-killers? Or are you surrounded by positive and inspiring people?

FIND SUCCESSFUL PEOPLE WHO INSPIRE AND MOTIVATE YOU TO ACHIEVE YOUR GOALS, NO MATTER HOW BIG YOUR VISION IS.

You can tell a lot about an individual by the things that make them angry, the things they focus on, and the ways they spend their time. Are they bitter, upset, or thinking of ways to beat down a competitor? Do they go on and on about small, meaningless, negative conflict and focus on the bad things that happen to them? Successful people do not think that way.

Eliminate the toxic people and naysayers who drag you down or make you feel bad. If you can't eliminate them, at least reduce the time you spend with those people. Don't surround yourself with negative people who are not motivating you each day. Find successful people who inspire and motivate you to achieve your goals, no matter how big your vision is.

> IT'S NOT ABOUT THE GRADES YOU MAKE AS MUCH AS IT IS ABOUT THE HANDS YOU SHAKE— CHERISH AND BUILD RELATIONSHIPS.
> –TONY JEARY

Find action-oriented people who have done what you want to do. These people are the momentum who will hold you accountable, yet also inspire you to achieve your true potential.

71.
Create and Nourish
a Life Team

Several of our past presidents have had a "kitchen cabinet," an informal group of trusted friends and associates who unofficially advised them on matters of state. They have historically been friends, allies, and great thinkers who have influenced policies and decisions during late-night talks and over rounds of golf. In return, they saw national changes influenced by their beliefs and passions, or had their careers arc and change for the better.

> THERE IS GREAT VALUE IN SURROUNDING YOURSELF WITH ALL KINDS OF PEOPLE TO HELP YOU DO LIFE.

There is great value in surrounding yourself with all kinds of people to help you do life. If you think about it, you most likely have these people around you already. But are there enough? Are they the right kind? Are you nourishing them?

We use the term *Life Team*, which is a hand-picked group of smart, talented individuals who have specific areas of expertise to leverage on your behalf. Whether advisors or doers, all are important. When you have a well-rounded life team, it's an easy matter to call someone who has the knowledge, expertise, or connections you need. You can also rely on these people to do the things you are not good at or don't like to do. This allows you to better invest energy doing the things you enjoy and excel in.

I (Tony) leverage an entire team that helps me achieve far better results by complementing my strengths with their expertise. My team is made up of several groups of people and includes home–life teamers like an electrician, a roofer, a landscaper, a painter, a plumber, and a builder. I also have a professional and handpicked office staff, writers, a videographer, a graphic artist, a couple of drivers, a pilot, a maid, and a gardener. Additionally, I have people on my team who support my family and me with their friendship and expert counsel and advice. These include life coaches, lawyers, bankers, a CPA, my pastor, financial advisors, an insurance agent, a literary agent, a strategist, and even trusted colleagues like a forum or an informal board.

> **BECOME A PERSON WHO IS WILLING TO CONSTANTLY GIVE, SHARE, AND CREATE VALUE FOR OTHERS.**
> **–TONY JEARY**

Having a powerful life team requires an intentional decision to put together a team of people you can go to when you want to grow, think, and get stuff done. If you have a problem, issue, or need, you can go and ask for advice, help, support, or action.

In order to understand who the players on your team should be, you really have to have a clear-cut vision of your goals in every category. Some people on your team will be mentors, others will simply be professional colleagues, and some will be executors. Be a person who can move mountains because you have built, assembled, appreciated, and nourished a power team of people around you.

72.
Jockeys Are More Important Than the Horses

This rule is simple: Always make sure that the right guy is on the team. Think of your company and the concept, as the horse. The people running it are the jockeys and if you put the wrong jockey on the horse, it won't get anywhere. The people you are going to be involved with in a project are much more important than the project itself.

> **THE PEOPLE YOU ARE GOING TO BE INVOLVED WITH IN A PROJECT ARE MUCH MORE IMPORTANT THAN THE PROJECT ITSELF.**

If you're a high achiever, chances are you've got a sixth sense that affords you the ability to read people well. Focus on the most important traits in people you do business with such as integrity, honesty, and a strong work ethic. If they don't have those traits, it's a pretty safe bet that they're not good jockeys.

One of the most famous jockeys that ever lived was George Edward Arcaro. Eddie, as he was known to millions of his fans, is one of only two men to win five Kentucky Derbies. In all, Eddie won seventeen Triple Crown races and two Triple Crowns. Eddie was the leading money winner three times. When he retired in 1962, he had won 549 stakes races and over $30 million—both records. What is overlooked about his extraordinary career is that he lost 250 races in a row before ever riding a winner. He had a character trait of strength and persistence. And that's the kind of person you want on your team.

Make the right choices about people when you're doing a deal or put-

> DISCOVER AND BE
> AWARE OF WHAT
> OTHERS REALLY WANT
> AND CARE ABOUT.
> –TONY JEARY

ting together your business strategy. If you don't have a good feel for the people after the initial meeting, or in a business deal, don't do the project, no matter how attractive it may be. Don't put a bad jockey on a good horse.

73.
You Can't Do a Good Deal with a Bad Guy

You can't have a good deal with a bad guy. Sometimes entrepreneurs are looking so hard for a deal that they overlook the people who brought the deal to the table. If you like a project but don't like the people that come with it, don't do the deal. You don't need the headaches.

> IF YOU LIKE A PROJECT BUT DON'T LIKE THE PEOPLE THAT COME WITH IT, DON'T DO THE DEAL. YOU DON'T NEED THE HEADACHES.

If you're in doubt, build specific out parameters into the deal or performance clauses, in case the deal goes sideways. But the best solution is to know how you feel up front.

Winston Churchill said, "Dogs look up to you, cats look down on you. Give me a pig. He just looks you in the eye and treats you as an equal." I (Peter) took that message to heart. In my book, *Never Fight with a Pig*, I said, "Never engage in senseless battles. Never allow yourself to lose sight of your goals and engage in needless conflict or hassles that provoke you. Why bring negative energy into your world?"

Make sure your business deals are equal. Don't go in fighting to win, at the expense of everyone else. Remember that this rule doesn't just apply to the person you're doing business with; it includes their entire organization.

> IF YOU ARE NOT IN OVER YOUR HEAD, YOU'RE NOT IN!
> –PETER THOMAS

You don't want to deal with a bad guy, so don't. But you've also got to be a good person to do deals with. Be the person others want to work with, the one they'd seek to do a deal with because you've built a reputation of integrity and success. The best scenario is a win-win situation for you both.

74.
Build Relationships and Help Others Win

Most high achievers admit they could not have begun their journey without the encouragement, support, and advice of the people around them. This is true for you, too, right? Remember that success is often built on a series of connecting relationships. No matter what your industry is, you will be dealing with others to buy, sell, and promote. You can't do it alone, no matter how smart you are. John Donne spoke the truth when he wrote, "No man is an island." We're all a part of something larger than ourselves, and we are interconnected in a way that assures our success only when we fully accept our interconnectedness.

> **SUCCESS IS OFTEN BUILT ON A SERIES OF CONNECTING RELATIONSHIPS.**

Often people in business focus solely on the people they want to do business with, yet neglect the people around them. But they're losing out, because sometimes it's the people close to them who are the key to unlocking the next door, and we're not just talking about gatekeepers. There are seemingly innocuous people you may encounter in life or in business who you would be surprised about if you knew their connections.

Build relationships by having a genuine approach and by appreciating others. Treat strangers, business associates, and others with care. Talk, listen, and nurture your relationships because they are equity. People will help make deals happen and endorse you and your business.

Each time you make a new contact, ask yourself, "How can I nourish that relationship? How can I give this person something of value? How can I do more than is expected to help him or her win?" I (Tony) have my team log new contacts into our database and catalog it in a way that will help us connect with the person in a meaningful way. When you help those around you win, they will, in turn, want to help you win. It's fairly simple to do, and reaps huge benefits for all stakeholders.

> SOMETIMES THE GREATEST SUCCESS CAN BE MEASURED BY THE NUMBER OF PEOPLE YOU INFLUENCE AND ENCOURAGE IN THEIR PURSUIT OF SUCCESS.
> –TONY JEARY

We encourage you to sit down and make a list of all the key people around you. Then be more intentional about nurturing those relationships and asking for their help in reaching your goals. Make it a two-way street, and ask what you can do for them, as well. You may start moving toward your goals a lot faster!

75.
Listen Up!

In business, listening is a critical skill. People who don't listen often miss key indicators, clues, and components that drive the sale, as well as important opportunities. They aren't in touch with anyone's needs but their own.

Listening well can make the difference between success and failure. You can't do a good business deal if you aren't armed with all the facts. And the only way to understand everything is to listen carefully. Sometimes you'll gain new information that radically changes the direction of your decision. Listening is the key to excellent decision-making.

Think about how you feel when someone appears like they're not listening to you. There is no greater sign of disrespect than ignoring someone's needs, words, or wishes. When someone does not listen to their husband or wife, the relationship disintegrates. When someone doesn't listen to their teenager, they can miss very important clues, major life events, or issues that need attention. When

> PEOPLE WHO DON'T LISTEN OFTEN MISS KEY INDICATORS, CLUES, AND COMPONENTS THAT DRIVE THE SALE, AS WELL AS IMPORTANT OPPORTUNITIES.

someone does not listen to their boss, they can miss important details on a project or misinterpret what that person needs. When someone doesn't listen to a prospective client, the client notices and wants to take their business elsewhere.

In the *Strategic Acceleration* Studio we have a unique way of letting our clients know we are listening. In fact, the entire studio session is built around listening. Our listening tools are a projector where the client information and ideas are projected onto a screen for everyone sitting around the conference table to see. We have a full-time assistant throughout the day who takes notes and catalogs the ideas offered up in the room. But we go much deeper than just note-taking. We have a specific proprietary matrix document that contains the name of every individual in the room. During the meeting, we ask each person to contribute and we write down exactly what they said on the matrix document. At the end of each session, we go around the room to each and every individual and ask them for their specific opinion on the day and our process, and how they perceived it to be valuable for them. When a client is asked this question, they give you positive feedback. Instead of saying goodbye and wondering how the people in the room received our coaching session, we actually get their feedback live. It's a very good process for strengthening the bond with the client and building credibility.

Listening involves concentration and contribution. You must have concentration to actually hear the information and the point the person talking is conveying. It requires concentration to block out distracting thoughts and discipline to refrain from speaking when you have something to say. Contribution should only come after the person talking has adequately communicated their ideas. Then when it's appropriate to contribute, you can add to the conversation or ignite a spark that will offer solutions and ideas.

76.
Focus on People
of Influence

A great rule is to identify, focus on, and nurture the eight to ten people in your life that have the most influence and impact over reaching your business objectives. Sometimes these people are customers or clients, sometimes they're key personnel, sometimes they may be a prospect, and sometimes they may be a strategic partner.

Being able to identify each of these people and their roles, and then being able to take the time to understand what their priorities and objectives are, puts you in a position to make sure those people are winning. In return, these people can provide what you need, whether it be intelligence, purchasing things, giving you support, or impacting any part of the priorities that you have running your business. It's an extraordinary advantage to have identified your top people of influence. (You can even list them in your phone or tablet, along with what's important to them.)

> IDENTIFY, FOCUS ON, AND NURTURE THE EIGHT TO TEN PEOPLE IN YOUR LIFE THAT HAVE THE MOST INFLUENCE AND IMPACT OVER REACHING YOUR BUSINESS OBJECTIVES.

If you really want to get very specific with each of these people, discover what their top one or two priorities are so that you might support them with even more focus. Having that clarity and synergy can greatly impact the extraordinary results you desire.

IX. MONEY

"Business opportunities are like buses,
there's always another one coming."
– RICHARD BRANSON

"There's class warfare, all right, but it's my class, the rich class,
that's making war, and we're winning."
- WARREN BUFFETT

"Too many people spend money they earned . . . to buy things they
don't want . . . to impress people that they don't like."
- WILL ROGERS

77.
Win Big
(or at Least Lose Small)

Sometimes you're going to win and sometimes you're going to lose. As long as the losses are small, you will be okay.

Successful individuals have a tolerance for this and understand that you're not always going to hit a home run. The key is not to lose too big, since big losses can wipe out assets and eat up any profits you may have gained. Assess your risk and only invest your time, resources, and energy in projects where it's expected that you'll lose small and win big. When you do lose, you can assess the situation in order to not repeat the same mistake twice. And, it's important to use your own common sense and business acumen. In business, it's nice to win big but it's more important to lose small, and often, so long as you're learning from it. You will never learn how *not* to lose (or even how to lose gracefully), but you'll recognize the factors that contributed to the loss and how to spot them in the future.

> SUCCESSFUL INDIVIDUALS UNDERSTAND THAT YOU'RE NOT ALWAYS GOING TO HIT A HOME RUN.

When I (Peter) was negotiating the rights of the Century 21 Real Estate Franchise rights for Canada, our team had all of the negotiating done and agreed to reconvene the next day to conclude the transaction. That evening I tried to work out the numbers to see just how good this investment could be. Century 21 had a similar regional franchise agreement that they used with every group. I could not afford to pay them as much as the other regions because my region was different, but how could I explain that and still acquire the rights to what I felt would be the best deal I had ever done? I loved the project but felt that there should be an accommodation for the uniqueness of the Canadian Region.

I explained that Canada was a very big country, bigger than the continental U.S. In fact, we would be better described as a country that was 4,500 miles long and only 100 miles high, because that was where most of the population was. There was no region in the U.S. for Century 21 that was anywhere near the size.

Because of the size of the region, I argued that it would be so much more expensive to service that we could not afford to pay the fees that the other regions paid. With this presentation of the facts, the Century 21 principals bought the argument, and I received a one-third discount of the fees to compensate for the size of the country. That was a big win. Many years later when this company was sold, its value was substantially more than any other region in the system. Of course a lot of the reason for the high value was the extraordinary job done by the management and the staff of the company, but in addition to the excellent management job, the fact that we had more left on our bottom line increased our value substantially.

In business, remember to focus on winning. What you focus on is what you'll get.

78.
Establish a Relationship With a Banker Who Likes You

If you're an entrepreneur who has ever tried to secure a loan from a bank, you are well aware of the challenges and frustrations that this process can pose. If you have never had a good banking relationship, it's time to get one.

> **IF YOU HAVE NEVER HAD A GOOD BANKING RELATIONSHIP, IT'S TIME TO GET ONE.**

Some banks are very large and complex entities, and getting any kind of assistance requires jumping through hoops and filling out mountains of paperwork. There's a process to everything, but the bigger the bank, the bigger the process. Traditional banks have traditional goals. If you're an entrepreneur, find a banker with an entrepreneur mindset.

An entrepreneurial banker will not be so caught up in process flow. They will view your deal with an entrepreneurial mindset, and you will have a greater chance of success if you choose someone who thinks the way you do. Choose the right players to fuel and fund your goals, and begin building essential relationships. This includes the right banker.

79.
Put Your Understanding of the Deal in Writing

Be sure you have clarity concerning all expectations when you are making a deal. If you don't read the fine print, it's your fault.

Before and even after you have completed a deal, write down your understanding of the terms in a business letter format, if it isn't already clearly written in a contract supported by both sides. This document will uncover any misunderstandings immediately and set out expectations for everyone involved.

> IF YOU DON'T READ THE FINE PRINT, IT'S YOUR FAULT.

Often people hear two different things in the same conversation. Each person hears what's important to them, and that's natural. You want to prevent wasted time and energy or busted deals later by reiterating what you believe was agreed upon, to keep everyone on the same page, strengthen relationships, and move forward. End every meeting by saying, "I will get back to you in writing as to my understanding of the deal." Or, do as I (Tony) do: Have a team member take notes during the meeting or phone call, putting all expectations and action items in a document that will be emailed to all parties immediately after the meeting.

80.
Pay Average Salaries and Higher Bonuses

EXPECT EXCELLENCE IN ACCORDANCE WITH THE LEVEL OF COMPENSATION.

Most successful people surround themselves with like-minded people who are vested in their success almost as much as they are, whose values complement their own, and whose expertise aligns with what is needed to reach their goals. To keep your great players committed long-term, pay them in a way that shows them how important they are to you and share the wealth when results are achieved. Research your industry and know the average pay. Then be creative with bonuses so with great results, people get paid more than virtually anywhere else they can plug into.

If you want to create true "partnerships," pay people in a way that makes them believe their expertise is valued and that they have everything to win by staying engaged with you. If constructed properly, when other team members are winning, you will be winning at an exponential rate. Expect excellence in accordance with the level of compensation. When you do this, all stakeholders win.

STRIP YOUR COMPANY OF CASH FROM TIME TO TIME SO THAT YOU BECOME PERSONALLY RICH AS WELL AS CORPORATELY RICH.
–TONY JEARY

81.
Keep Your Will Current

Part of designing your own life is having a say in what happens once you're gone. That includes having a will and keeping it current. Remember that a will isn't just about money; your will should represent a snapshot of how you want your businesses to run, what charities you want to honor, what assets you want to leave your loved ones, and how they are all to be distributed.

Use your lawyer for legal advice. Select a trusted mentor or advisor to act as a trustee in the event of your death, and keep that trustee current with your business operations. Prepare a thorough package on all of your companies and assets annually, and review it with your trustee. We urge you to appreciate the importance of this so it will leave nothing to chance once you've passed.

> A WILL ISN'T JUST ABOUT MONEY; YOUR WILL SHOULD REPRESENT A SNAPSHOT OF HOW YOU WANT YOUR BUSINESSES TO RUN, WHAT CHARITIES YOU WANT TO HONOR, WHAT ASSETS YOU WANT TO LEAVE YOUR LOVED ONES, AND HOW THEY ARE ALL TO BE DISTRIBUTED.

82.
Pay All Small Suppliers on Time

> SMALL VENDORS CAN BE SOME OF YOUR BIGGEST ASSETS—THEY ARE EAGER TO KEEP YOUR BUSINESS AND WILL WORK ON YOUR TIMING VERSUS THEIR OWN.
> –PETER THOMAS

Become a big customer to your smaller suppliers, and pay them on time. Small vendors can be some of your biggest assets—they are eager to keep your business and will work on your timing versus their own. They count on timely payments more than the big guys, and you will remain a high priority to them when everybody wins.

In addition, care about their success. Make them feel valued and help them win. Refer others to them and let them know you do so. You will be at the top of their list to please when you place new orders with them. If you are good to them, pay them on time, and refer others to them, they will be a huge part of your support system.

Contract out all tasks you can afford that are feasible. Trade money for time.

83.
Make Others
Feel Significant

There's a big difference between appreciating people and making them feel significant. Of course, you want to appreciate others. But even more than that, you need to make those important people in your life feel significant.

> MAKE PEOPLE
> FEEL SIGNIFICANT.
> PEOPLE BLOSSOM
> UNDER APPROVAL,
> COMPLIMENTS, AND
> FEELING LOVED . . .
> APPRECIATE WHAT
> YOU WANT MORE OF
> PERSONALLY.
>
> –TONY JEARY

Success typically comes in your life (both personally and professionally) by others who fill gaps for you and who are your cheerleaders and top supporters. There is rarely an exception to this. Think of those people in your own life. Do you make those people feel like they're significant? Do you brag on them in the presence of others? Do you give others credit? Do you ask for other people's opinions on things important to you and to the success of your company? Are you interested in the things that matter to them?

From a client standpoint, what are you doing to make them feel special and significant? I (Tony) have a standard I call the "black card" standard. Achieving *Black Card Level* is the most elite level, and it comes with special treatment. This is what we want to be known for—giving others the black card treatment. We pick our clients up and drive

> DO YOU GIVE OTHERS CREDIT? DO YOU ASK FOR OTHER PEOPLE'S OPINIONS ON THINGS IMPORTANT TO YOU AND TO THE SUCCESS OF YOUR COMPANY?

them to our meetings, we offer our resources at no extra charge, we create a spa-like atmosphere in the restroom, we have an outside lounge where people can gather at break times, we offer up healthy snacks and drinks, we print their boarding passes, and we even sometimes wash their vehicles if they've driven themselves. We want our clients to feel like we are their concierge service and that all the details matter—that they matter.

How can you do the same for people who are special in your life?

X. WEALTH

"Experience taught me a few things. One is to listen to your gut, no matter how good something sounds on paper. The second is that you're generally better off sticking with what you know. And the third is that sometimes your best investments are the ones you don't make."
– DONALD TRUMP

"Happiness is not in the mere possession of money; it lies in the joy of achievement, in the thrill of creative effort."
- FRANKLIN D. ROOSEVELT

"If we command our wealth, we shall be rich and free. If our wealth commands us, we are poor indeed."
- EDMUND BURKE

84.
Be Financially Strong

Have you developed good habits that model responsible behavior, and do you have a healthy attitude about money? Are you growing toward financial strength?

Being strong financially requires making sound intentional decisions. Make calculated risks that don't leave you too exposed. It includes building net worth as well as having good cash flow. Being strong financially will get you through the tough times that are bound to come when economies change, life changes, and circumstances happen that are often beyond your control.

> **BEING STRONG FINANCIALLY REQUIRES MAKING SOUND INTENTIONAL DECISIONS.**

When you aren't financially strong, you may be forced to make short-term decisions that aren't necessarily the right ones. If you are smart, have your money work for you, and keep your personal recourse debt ratio low, you'll take a tremendous amount of pressure off of yourself. Being strong financially is something within your control. It will help weather storms and allow you to make better decisions for your future.

85.
Don't Fall in Love
With an Asset

This rule involves the things you own. When it comes to business, you'll never be financially successful if you're too attached to the things you sell. You have to be unemotional; if you're too attached to something you won't sell it. Instead, you'll miss windows of opportunity.

> WHEN IT COMES TO BUSINESS, YOU'LL NEVER BE FINANCIALLY SUCCESSFUL IF YOU'RE TOO ATTACHED TO THE THINGS YOU SELL.

Understand what emotions and thoughts are driving you to keep hanging on to things that may be preventing growth. This rule also applies to business deals that have gone beyond their cycle of profitability. There is pain involved with detoxing (letting go), and sometimes you have to prune—let go of people, places, and things that don't serve you or your goals anymore. Don't emotionally keep "feeding" a bad deal. Do an audit on your partnerships, and assets.

Is it time to cut your losses? Is it time to let something go? It's much easier to move forward if you cut emotional ties.

86.
Be a Risk Assessor, Not a Risk Taker

Every entrepreneur takes risks and that, by definition, makes them a risk taker. However, the degree of risk is directly related to the due diligence one makes before pulling the trigger. If your diligence is what it should be, you will become a risk assessor, more than a risk taker.

IN BUSINESS DEALS, DON'T BE AFRAID TO DIG DEEP FOR ANSWERS IN ORDER TO ASSESS RISK.

When we look at a deal, we research it completely—inside and out—and consider the timing of it as well. If you don't look at the timing of the deal, you can still get the best deal, but at the wrong time. Timing is everything.

In business deals, don't be afraid to dig deep for answers in order to assess risk. Do you know everything you need to know? Always carry out a complete due diligence on the prospective deal, the people involved in the deal, and the finances of it.

There are four elements every business person should consider when doing their due diligence. They are:

1) People: Who are the people in the deal? Are they fun, capable, compatible, and brilliant?
2) Communication: How do they communicate? Are they guarding and hiding things, or are they open?
3) Timing: What's the timing of the deal? If someone invented a wheel or a telephone right now, they've missed the deal. The timing would be off. But if the deal is perfect and the timing is perfect,

you won't mind paying a little more for it.

4) Finance: If the people, communication, and timing are right, you'll always find the money.

> IF FRIENDS AND FAMILY ASK FOR CASH BECAUSE YOU ARE RICH, ONLY GIVE IT TO THEM AS A GIFT. DON'T EXPECT IT BACK.
> –TONY JEARY

Assess the risk but don't try to take risks. People think they're being courageous and bold by being risk takers. Because of that, we've seen a lot of stupid people who do risky deals. Great entrepreneurs are not risk takers. Contrary to popular belief, great entrepreneurs are risk assessors.

87.
Continually Upgrade the Size of Your Deals

FOCUS ON DOING DEALS THAT ARE BIGGER AND BETTER.

If you want to become wealthy, don't get satisfied with what you're earning today. Focus on doing deals that are bigger and better. Why not shoot for the stars? Whatever the size of the deals you are doing today, consider them small compared to what you will be doing in the future.

Use the size of your last deal as a benchmark for future deals, and think much bigger next time. Plan for growth.

88.
Inspect Before Acquisition

Fund the purchase of any acquisition only after you or one of your key people has personally inspected the tentative purchase (company, property, asset—it doesn't matter). A visual inspection can be critical to ascertain the true value and opportunity of the investment. This lesson was learned the hard way by both of us!

I (Tony) bought a house one time from just a picture of the front, only to discover the entire back was burned out. Wow, that was a surprise. And I (Peter) bought 13 units in a townhouse and it turned out that there were only 12. That's an 8 percent hit right from the start.

If it sounds too good to be true, inspect it. If there is no time to inspect the acquisition, it may be a better play to pass on the opportunity, even if it turns out to be a good one. There are always other deals and opportunities.

> FUND THE PURCHASE OF ANY ACQUISITION ONLY AFTER YOU OR ONE OF YOUR KEY PEOPLE HAS PERSONALLY INSPECTED THE TENTATIVE PURCHASE.

XI. EXECUTE

*"If you are not willing to risk the unusual,
you will have to settle for the ordinary."*
– JIM ROHN

*"Action may not always bring happiness,
but there is no happiness without action. "*
- WILLIAM JAMES

*"We cannot live for ourselves alone. Our lives are connected by a
thousand invisible threads, and along these sympathetic fibers, our
actions run as causes and return to us as results."*
- HERMAN MELVILLE

89.
Speed Matters:
Accelerate Results

We have collectively studied the subject of accelerated growth and success for years. The work I (Tony) specifically do on behalf of clients is focused on helping them grow their enterprises faster. But why is speed so important?

> **GET THE BUSINESS BEFORE SOMEONE ELSE GETS A CHANCE TO GET IN THE DOOR AND GIVE THEIR COMPETING SALES PRESENTATION.**

Business is a results contest, and that typically involves competition. In today's world, the winner is usually whoever delivers their products better and faster. In other words, the winners consistently get the *right* results faster than their competition.

When we talk about getting the right results, we're talking about the kind of results that are planned in advance and are achieved on purpose. This means the right results are outcomes that were foreseen as part of turning a vision into reality. Successful people, by this definition, know the outcomes they need in advance, and they also know how to make them happen.

Successful people (and organizations) have three strategic distinctions that produce the right results faster:

1. They have clarity about what they want.
2. They know how to focus on doing the things that matter.

3. They know how to execute their plans and achieve their goals.

Regarding speed, there are examples throughout history in business where one company beat another to market and it was a game changer. If you don't think speed matters, look at technology such as Facebook. Anyone could create Facebook, but now that it's created it has such a huge following that people are loyal to it because that's where their friends are. It's the same thing with LinkedIn. It's just a database and anyone could build it, but LinkedIn and Facebook made it happen.

Timing is also a big deal and often times the first one to the prospective buyer is the one who gets the business, because they're meeting the feeling of a need or of a perceived need. Get the business before someone else gets a chance to get in the door and give their competing sales presentation.

Speed matters, especially in today's fast-paced society.

90.
Have a "Get It Done Now" Mindset

Stop making excuses and get it done! Quite simply, the difference between successful and unsuccessful people is that successful people achieve predetermined results. You cannot execute, achieve, and make results happen without being really clear about what you want.

One essay that so clearly captures the essence of this rule is the famous "Message to Garcia." In 1899, Elbert Hubbard wrote a best¬selling inspirational essay entitled "A Message to Garcia" about a courier named Rowan. Rowan, upon request from President William McKinley, braved the hostile Cuban wilderness on foot to deliver a message to Calixto García, a rebel leader also involved in tensions with Spain. When tasked with the mission, Rowan asked no questions, gave no argument, and offered no concerns; he simply left, disappeared for three weeks, and did what was asked of him. After this essay was published, the phrase "take a message to Garcia" became a common colloquial for having initiative and getting the job done. Every leader loves people who get things done. Right?

What if you were that man or woman charged with such an important task? Are you capable and willing and do you have the ability to execute? Do you just think about doing it, or are you actually doing it?

It's the earliest version of Nike's philosophy: "Just Do It." Indeed, when we are acting on a request or striving to reach a personal objective, is there any other approach to even consider? Just do it. Get it done. Focus, power through, and succeed. Value a capacity for independent action, moral intelligence, a strength of will, and a willingness to cheerfully catch hold and lift.

When you're next faced with a task, project, assignment, big meeting, you name it—either for yourself or on behalf of another—take action. Start at the beginning and deploy High Leverage Activities (HLAs) to get the most out of your action, effort, and resources (see #47). If you feel stuck, commit to even fifteen minutes of action; you'll see that you often get caught up in the task and make tremendous progress.

> **THE DIFFERENCE BETWEEN SUCCESSFUL AND UNSUCCESSFUL PEOPLE IS THAT SUCCESSFUL PEOPLE ACHIEVE PREDETERMINED RESULTS.**

Your colleagues, owners, clients, shareholders, and board will value this attention to action and commitment to overcoming whatever obstacles, uncertainties, or questions surround the task in front of you.

Let your brand grow and more and more people will count on you to get things done, to succeed where they cannot, and to not clutter delegation by creating more issues, excuses, and mental roadblocks. Personally and professionally, become someone people can rely upon. This is creating a reputation of execution, and it is just as valuable now as it was 114 years ago.

Go forward and create your powerful mindset, your reputation of execution. This will increase your personal success, since creating wins for others makes you indispensable.

91.
Production Before Perfection

Everyone procrastinates from time to time, but sometimes entire organizations get stuck and fail to move quickly with their execution. One big reason for this is the need to be perfect. People freeze. They stop. They fail to move forward due to self-talk that says, "It's not good enough," or "Let me get it in better shape before I do."

We believe very strongly that a culture that really fosters, encourages, and reinforces the idea of getting things going in motion and then polishing as you go is a huge win to execution. There's a competitive advantage when you no longer have to be perfect in order to make progress. How's your organization with this? How are you with this? Do you have to have things perfect before you move to the next step? Generally speaking, in business Production Before Perfection (PBP) can be a huge deal (see #32).

> **AVOID PROCRASTINATION AND GET FASTER RESULTS. FOCUS ON STARTING INSTEAD OF FINISHING AND THEN ADJUST AS YOU GO.**
> —TONY JEARY

We encourage people to first be aware of the idea that people can get stuck sometimes. Leaders can get stuck, which can then paralyze the organization. As leaders, we want to make sure that we are getting people moving (including ourselves), and the whole culture wins.

92.
Execute with Accountability!

Clarity and focus are nothing without execution. Execution is doing. Executing with speed is to accelerate action. When you have clarity, you know what you want to achieve. You are able to put it in writing and you are able to specifically communicate the "why" of it to those you need to work with to execute the vision. When you and your team have this ability, it is the result of having what I call "Strategic Clarity." How clear are you about what you really want? Our research and experience with hundreds of top performers indicates that most people have less clarity than they think they have. As a result they have difficulty pulling their teams together and frequently get the wrong results.

The distinction for getting the right results faster is execution. You can create the greatest plan in the world and establish the most focused goals imaginable, but if you fail to execute the plan you will not achieve it. Every business has at least one strategic plan in its file cabinet that never became a reality.

What is the biggest reason plans fail to be executed?

> YOU CAN CREATE THE GREATEST PLAN IN THE WORLD AND ESTABLISH THE MOST FOCUSED GOALS IMAGINABLE, BUT IF YOU FAIL TO EXECUTE THE PLAN YOU WILL NOT ACHIEVE IT.

By far the biggest culprit is a communication disconnect between those who conceive the vision and those who must turn it into reality. You want execution to ensure clarity and leverage peer accountability. This happens by constantly sharing the action lens in front of your team, discussing what's done and what's not. Pretty simple and yet powerfully effective.

Invariably, when businesses conduct internal effectiveness surveys, poor communication is usually one of the top three problems identified. To achieve the right results faster, leaders must continually cascade their vision down through the organization (small or large) so that every team member understands and supports it. This is not an easy thing to do and is the reason so many organizations struggle with it. Communication problems and challenges are found in every nook and cranny of our lives, from meetings to email, from text to voicemail. Each communication challenge impacts execution.

> *STRATEGIC CLARITY* IS ACHIEVED WHEN YOU HAVE A CLEAR VIEW OF YOUR VISION AND UNDERSTAND WHAT YOU REALLY WANT, WHY YOU WANT IT, THE VALUE OF DOING IT, AND THE HIGHEST PURPOSE FOR DOING IT.
>
> –TONY JEARY

Though clarity, focus, and execution are strongly linked and all three are important, the most significant is execution because execution is about doing. Clarity and focus provide a roadmap for the basis for doing what you need to do, but execution is about actually doing it, and this is where you will spend the bulk of your time.

Regardless of your role or vision, you we all know we need others' assistance and cooperation to be highly successful; and your ability to persuade has a lot to do with others' willingness not only to assist you, but also to exceed expectations. When you can persuade others to exceed expectations, you take execution to a higher level and really move the results needle. The most successful people can effectively convince and persuade other people to take action on their behalf.

93.
Measure Everything—
Measurement Matters

If you really want to perform as a leader at the top level, or in any other area of your life, you need written targets and you need to measure progress against those targets. In order for top performers to be their very best, they can start with a simple assessment centered around leadership best practices to create real focus and results that matter. Assessments can measure leadership ability, time management, meeting effectiveness, or any other objective.

Want to move to the mastery level of getting results? You need to take to heart that measurement matters. This is probably not an earth-shattering concept. Recognizing and being aware of this is one thing; really leveraging it as a tool to be your very best is something even more powerful. Challenge yourself to take one or more areas of your life or business that could use improvement, and figure out what measurements matter to you. If you want to improve your health, maybe you'd measure your BMI, blood pressure, or waistline. Leadership skills could be measured by how well you strategically plan, prioritize, or deploy your team. You might want to improve your financial position, so you'd examine bank balances, P&Ls, investment worksheets, or other critical success fac-

> CHALLENGE YOURSELF TO TAKE ONE OR MORE AREAS OF YOUR LIFE OR BUSINESS THAT COULD USE IMPROVEMENT, AND FIGURE OUT WHAT MEASUREMENTS MATTER TO YOU.

tors.

Take a few minutes and jot down where you are and where you want to be. Get your team involved; your family involved. See for yourself how much measurement matters! Real measurement over and over means real results and will bring a whole new level of focus on measuring and refining.

94.
Results vs. Activity

People really get a lot of stuff done, but they don't always get the right stuff done. What you want to do is consistently communicate and foster an environment that rewards and recognizes, as a general rule, people getting results versus just having activity.

> CONSISTENTLY COMMUNICATE AND FOSTER AN ENVIRONMENT THAT REWARDS AND RECOGNIZES, AS A GENERAL RULE, PEOPLE GETTING RESULTS VERSUS JUST HAVING ACTIVITY.

Making lists—daily lists, weekly lists, even monthly lists—to be able to prove that the results are being accomplished is a huge win for a company. Results move things along. Having that philosophy from the beginning can be very powerful. Consider including this as one of your operating standards so that people see very clearly that you and your organization are after rewarding the result, not just doing stuff.

95.
Work the Plan, Utilize a Scorecard

One of the biggest issues surrounding execution is the failure of accountability. Failure of accountability leads to people not taking action.

We recommend you take your plan and build it into a scorecard system where (as simple as it sounds), people's names are connected to specific actions. Whether they be tactics or strategies, there are actions that need to be deployed to be able to make the scorecard come to life and the results happen.

> HAVING A SCORECARD ALSO ALLOWS EACH PERSON TO VISUALLY SEE HOW THEIR PIECE FITS INTO THE OVERALL SUCCESS OF THE PLAN.

Having a scorecard also allows each person to visually see how their piece fits into the overall success of the plan. A great rule is for each plan to have a scorecard attached and an agreed-upon timeframe for completion. This allows for peer accountability, which supports proper execution.

XII. HEALTH

"The reason I exercise is for the quality of life I enjoy."
– KENNETH H. COOPER

"Every person has the right to look and feel like a million bucks."
- DR. OZ

"People are just as happy as they make up their minds to be."
- ABRAHAM LINCOLN

96.
Do Business in Places You Consider Enjoyable

High achievers need consistent inspiration to be their best. In order to give your best, you need to make sure you're taking care of yourself and that you're working in an environment that makes you happy. Determining what inspires you is a key to impacting your business and life success. Where do you work best? What makes you feel good?

> **IN ORDER TO GIVE YOUR BEST, YOU NEED TO MAKE SURE YOU'RE TAKING CARE OF YOURSELF AND THAT YOU'RE WORKING IN AN ENVIRONMENT THAT MAKES YOU HAPPY.**

When we first met to discuss this book, it was on Peter and his wife Rita's yacht in the middle of the day, surrounded by beauty. Lunch was served on the deck and we sat and brainstormed ideas that would help others thrive and build successful businesses. We could have had the meeting anywhere, like in a poorly lit conference room or a stuffy office, but instead we chose the back deck of a beautiful yacht off of Victoria Island in Canada! What a beautiful and inspiring setting it was, to launch a new project and cement friendships. But it didn't just happen unintentionally. There was planning involved and we had to block calendars. Ultimately the choice of location was worth it.

When I (Tony) discovered the power of environment, my life changed. Since that time I've been consistently curious about research, models, and best practices related to creating an inspiring work place. In today's world, the office is anywhere. It's completely up to you to decide how you want to position yourself. It's your life! (As I'm writing this section here, as an example, I'm on an American 777–300 from London to Dallas in my own mini bedroom.)

Where do you want to live and work? Do you want to build a business that's brick and mortar or fluid and mobile? I've done meetings in pools, mountains, hot tubs, yachts, tour buses, conference tables, and in lounge chairs in the back yard of my studio. I have the finest couches and chairs and even outdoor air conditioning. Every detail is relaxing, down to the candles, textures, and curtains. I designed it to be inspiring to others but also to me.

> BY SETTING GOALS THAT CREATE AND MAINTAIN A HEALTHIER BODY, YOU ARE TAKING STEPS THAT CAN LITERALLY BENEFIT YOU FOR A LIFETIME.
> –TONY JEARY

Think of your work and personal life as the same thing, not as separate entities. After all you should love what you do and do what you love, and that includes where you work! The location is just as important as the work you're performing. If you're locked up in an office every day and you don't have any fresh air, chances are you not going to like your work for very long.

Inspiration comes from beautiful people and surroundings, so you might as well work somewhere that you love and with people you enjoy. The choice is, of course, yours.

97.
Live Healthy!

Truly successful people live healthy, eat well, exercise, manage stress, rest, relax, de-stress, and breathe well with deep breathing exercises. Healthy people understand their body and the triggers that lead to stress. They avoid those triggers, and work to incorporate a positive mental attitude and healthy positive habits into their life.

Do you understand your body? Do you know what foods make you feel tired, bloated, and fatigued and what foods lead to a healthy, energetic day? Do you know what foods have a high GI and cause you to store fat?

So many people don't. But when you begin to understand how your body works, reacts, and feels, you'll make better food choices. You'll know what foods

> YOU WANT TO BE FINANCIALLY HEALTHY, SURE. BUT YOU ALSO WANT TO BE PHYSICALLY, EMOTIONALLY, AND SPIRITUALLY HEALTHY.

are best for you and which ones to avoid. You'll know when you feel more energy, and you'll exercise at that time of day. You'll know when you think better, and more clearly, and you'll schedule work during those times. Understanding your mind and body is key, and then guess what—as a leader, your people will often follow you.

Successful people are attracted to healthy people. Why? Because people want more of what you have; if you're unhealthy they don't want it. It's pretty simple. After years of coaching high achievers to earn more, learn more, and get more results, one of the interesting commonalities I (Tony) observed is the need for a healthier life. Many entrepreneurs or CEOs neglect their mental and physical health when they're striving for financial success. Does that sound like you?

We have both been focused on health for a decade or more. Eventually after reaching financial success you get to a point where you become more focused on holistic success. You want to be financially healthy, sure. But you also want to be physically, emotionally, and spiritually healthy.

We have both written books about wellness. In my (Peter's) *LifePilot* program, I teach entrepreneurs how to advance and excel creating clarity of values, and then use my own example of health. And I (Tony) wrote a book called *Ultimate Health* to help me mentor and coach others to success in the area of physical wellness. In order to live a healthier life in all quadrants, you have to pay attention to those things that matter.

> A HEALTHY BODY IS THE START TO A HEALTHY MIND AND A HEALTHY SOUL.
> –PETER THOMAS

Living healthy also means aligning your values to your daily activities. Get complete clarity on what you want and then live your life that way.

98.
Maintain a Strong Mental Mindset

What goes on in your mind truly impacts your health. Assess your own self-talk daily, and your beliefs about life. Understand your outlook. Is it positive? Adopt a willingness to release grudges and forgive, while focusing on the positives. Filter the input you receive from sources such as news, media, and negative people.

> **ASSESS YOUR OWN SELF-TALK DAILY, AND YOUR BELIEFS ABOUT LIFE. UNDERSTAND YOUR OUTLOOK. IS IT POSITIVE?**

Health for your mind includes being conscious about eliminating toxins such as unproductive thought patterns, unhealthy habits, and negative, self-limiting beliefs; and increasing positive thoughts, energy, and momentum. It encompasses being intentional about who you spend time with because the people around you greatly impact your success.

Think of the process of managing your mindset the same way you think of managing your business. If you owned a company, you wouldn't leave clutter all over the front office for your clients to see. The clutter would give an appearance of disarray, distraction, and disorganization. Why, then, would you want that in your personal space? There are ways to elevate your mindset on a daily basis to continually remind you of the positives in your life—but this takes intention.

Surround yourself with positive images and affirmations. Put photographs or objects in your office or home that remind you of positive moments, achievements, and memories. Be intentional about every photograph and every space—even down to what is in each photo. Each one should keep positive thoughts flowing. Keep your environment clear of unnecessary reminders of the negative aspects of life that can clutter your mind. Leave those details for administrative team members so these details are not sapping your creativity, production, or focus.

> YOU ONLY GET ONE LIFE TO LIVE, BUT IF YOU LIVE IT RIGHT, ONE LIFE IS ALL YOU NEED.
>
> –PETER THOMAS

Another important factor to a positive mindset is to keep healthy people in your space. We become like those around us, so spend time with quality individuals. Vow to make every room you enter a happier space simply because you are there. Make sure you are one of those people who others feed off of to authentically improve their self-confidence, their life, and their success; doing so will impact your own.

99.
Live Ultimate Longevity

You can live to be one hundred. You can live to be an active, healthy, and vibrant centenarian or even super centenarian, depending upon how dedicated you are to achieving ultimate health and reversing the effects of aging. If you take on a thoughtful and active role in your own well-being, and have regular wellness screenings, you should expect to live longer, and stronger, than the average person. The benefits are too important to ignore, because the quality of your remaining decades is largely dependent on your physical health.

Aging can be an amazing process and not a destructive one. You can literally thrive, start a new chapter in your life, and challenge yourself to new limits. You can age gracefully, continue to learn new things, and take on a new hobby, sport, or career, even if others around you have stopped moving, dreaming, and doing. Your life can be completely different than the average person. You can move into your next decades with vitality and an anything-is-possible mindset.

AS A GENERAL RULE, IT IS ALMOST ALWAYS EASIER AND LESS EXPENSIVE TO PREVENT DISEASE THAN IT IS TO TREAT IT ONCE HEALTH IS LOST.

As a general rule, it is almost always easier and less expensive to prevent disease than it is to treat it once health is lost. The difference between health care (preventive medicine) and sick care (going to the doctor after you feel bad) is testing, prevention, and a holistic mindset about your health. Although most people believe they are involved in their health care, it really is health carelessness when you wait until you feel pain or sickness to go and try to find a solution.

Shift your mind-set about the aging process and know that you have more control over aging than you think. Here's a powerful thought—you can look at age three ways: chronological, physical, and mental. With a chronological view you gain wisdom. With a physical view, you can actually preserve or actually reverse age with the right discipline. And with a mental view, you have that choice of going in reverse as well. You can play with your five-year-old and mentally enjoy kid games and other fun activities. You can also learn to enjoy your time, sitting on a bench and reflecting, putting your mind at rest and in reflect mode. Winning starts with awareness and that's true for health. Be aware; then take action.

> YOU CAN LIVE A PHYSICAL AGE THAT IS LESS THAN YOUR CHRONOLOGICAL AGE; IT STARTS WITH CLARITY OF WHAT YOU WANT.
> –TONY JEARY

Ultimately surround yourself intentionally and smartly with the right people. Having a team that acts as a strong support system to help you stay on top of your health is a major step toward powerful life management.

100.
Manage Stress

One of the major causes of disease, aging, and death is stress. Stress occurs when our mental, physical, or spiritual challenges exceed our ability to cope with them. Stress kills—literally. And it kills morale, too. On the personal side, it causes your body to secrete hormones that can have a negative impact on your health. On the organizational side, stress can cause turnover, burnout, and can even weaken execution.

When you can reduce stress, everything flows much more smoothly. Your business life, your relationships, and your physical well-being will all improve. Stress can be situational and caused by several factors, including how we plan, react, and cope with what we allow in our lives.

There will always be obstacles and issues in life that are outside your control. But those are externally driven, isolated events. Stress is what happens when pressure builds in the gap between the things we want to do

> STRESS IS WHAT HAPPENS WHEN PRESSURE BUILDS IN THE GAP BETWEEN THE THINGS WE WANT TO DO AND THE THINGS WE ARE ACTUALLY DOING.

and the things we are actually doing. It results from a lack of congruence between the life you want, your goals, and the life you live.

The best way to cure stress is to drill down to the source of the problem, and cut stress out before it even happens. If you do an "audit" and make a list of the top ten most stressful things that happen on a daily basis, you will begin to discover a lot of opportunities to make a difference. By changing certain habits, you can often eliminate most sources of stress in your life.

Your true wealth is determined by the amount of things you do not have to worry about. Worry is a stressor. Often, the most frequent stressor in anyone's life is a lack of time. But a lack of time is not actually producing the stress; it is the way you are managing your time. In that moment of rushing, you are stressed because you have a lack of time. But in the moments leading up to it, you had plenty. Building "margin time" into your life right now is one of the fastest ways to eliminate stress. Another reason to build margin time is to make room for life's unexpected events. Without a built-in margin time, people feel pressed and stressed. You owe it to yourself to live as stress free as possible.

> ELIMINATE STRESS; YOUR TRUE WEALTH IS DETERMINED BY THE AMOUNT OF THINGS YOU DO NOT HAVE TO WORRY ABOUT.
> —TONY JEARY

CONCLUSION

Love your life!

We love our lives. And it's not just because we're making money. We love making a positive impact, we love giving back to others, and we love doing deals. Although we have a lot of things in common, we also are two separate people living two different lives. Just like you we have specific things that we enjoy, such as hobbies or time with family, and we also have things that we don't like. Eliminating the negative and enhancing the positive is the key to loving each day.

Ask yourself what things in your world drag you down. What makes you feel bad? What makes you feel good? How do you want to give back to others? Part of loving your life is making a contribution to the lives of others. One of the hallmarks of centenarians is that they feel recognized and they are able to socially connect with others and give back to the world. Sometimes they give their time, and sometimes they give their energy, talent, wisdom, or resources. When you feel as if you're making a difference, you can't help but be excited about life.

Living an exciting, enthusiastic life is a decision. Some days can be difficult and some happy and adventurous, but once you have the right mindset and you decide to love your life, you will search for ways to learn more and ways to contribute to society. Through a lens of lifelong learning, lifelong loving, and lifelong giving, you will feel valued and strengthened. Look around. It's not hard to find someone in their 20s or 30s who seems less than enthusiastic about life, and it's not hard to find someone in their 80s or 90s who's very excited about life. It's not about your age, it's about your mindset, so don't let age limit you. No matter who you are, where you live, or how old you are, you can learn something new today that can add value and infuse energy and adrenaline into your life.

When you live enthusiastically, you'll be in flow. People places and things will be drawn to you. The opposite of that is that when you live in fear or hesitation, things will not be drawn to you and you'll feel like a victim. You'll have a scarcity mentality.

When you love your life, are clear on your values, and know the rules you want to live by, you're more motivated and inspired. You can lead with impact and draw people into your positive energy. It doesn't matter if they are contractors, vendors, partners, employees, or investors. People are drawn to people who do life well.

Be authentic and be self-aware. Audit yourself often. Even audit yourself against these 100 lessons. Become the best you that you can become. Live life intentionally.

ABOUT THE AUTHORS

Tony Jeary

Tony Jeary is a strategist. Many call him The RESULTS Guy ™ because of this simple fact—he helps clients get the right results faster. He is a unique and powerful facilitator and subject matter expert who has advised over 1,000 clients and published over 3 dozen books. His studio process of live note taking, combined with his *Strategic Acceleration* methodology, is a secret weapon for his special clients. Tony has invested the past 20 years developing facilitation processes and systems that allow him and his team to accelerate results, doing planning meetings in a single day, and producing results that often take days, weeks, and months in a single eight-hour session. That's a rare gift.

The world's greatest CEOs recognize the importance of thinking, strategy, and communication; and many seek Tony for all three of these. He's a gifted encourager who helps clarify visions.

The primary goal of every leader is to enhance value and communicate their vision effectively so that their teams can execute that vision in the marketplace. He does this, personally coaching presidents and CEOs of Walmart, TGI Friday's, New York Life, Firestone, Samsung, Ford, Texaco, and SAM's; even those on the Forbes richest 400 engage Tony for his advice. Tony personally helps these top leaders: define their goals; accelerate their opportunities; create, establish, and build their personal brands and careers; deliver powerful paradigm-shifting presentations; grow their leadership abilities; and accelerate the right results faster! He and/or his whole firm can be booked through his business manager. Tony Jeary International can be retained to do amazing things to support accelerated RESULTS. Learn more at www.tonyjeary.com.

Peter Thomas

Peter Thomas has been a serial entrepreneur for more than four decades, specializing in franchising and real estate. Peter is recognized as one of the leading developers and lenders of his time in North America. He has developed billions of dollars in real estate projects, from shopping centers, apartments, and condominiums, to golf courses.

Peter is the past Chairman and Founder of Century 21 Real Estate Canada Ltd., founded Samoth Capital Corporation, a Canadian public real estate company now known as Sterling Centrecorp Inc., and developed the Four Seasons Resort in Scottsdale, Arizona.

For his philanthropic contributions to society, Peter was recognized with the prestigious 2010 National Caring Award, an honor shared by Lance Armstrong, General Colin Powell, and Laura Bush.

Peter is the Chairman Emeritus of the Entrepreneurs' Organization and the bestselling author of two Canadian books, *Never Fight with a Pig* and *Be Great*. For further information please visit www.lifepilot.org.

Currently, Peter serves as Chairman and CEO of Thomas Franchise Solutions Ltd. and as a Director for the TFS Fund. Peter was very proud to be awarded his Honorary Doctorate of Laws LLD from the Royal Roads University in Victoria, British Columbia for his work with the creation of *LifePilot* (www.lifepilot.org) and for his other charity works.

What Can We Do For You

Strategic Acceleration

Let us work with you to develop a customized strategic plan for more clarity, focus, and execution, hence more accelerated results! We help people get the right results, faster.

Communication/Presentation Mastery™

Train (certify) your team to maximize every business opportunity, meeting and talk.

Results Coaching

Having coached the world's top CEOs and earners, Tony understands the need for speed in today's marketplace. Benefit from 20 years of best practices from the best of the best.

Strategic Acceleration Studio

Experience the *Strategic Acceleration* Studio and have at your fingertips two decades of best practices, processes, and tools for accelerating dramatic, sustained results in your organization.

Culture-Changing Webinars

Most organizations struggle with weekly meetings, poor email standards resulting in too many meetings and too many emails, costing valuable time. Results are dramatically being hurt because of people operating in overwhelm.

Tony has taken his expertise and developed simple 30-90 minute webinars that can save thousands of non-productive hours for an organization and greatly impact results. Let us discuss impacting your culture. Subjects include:

Email Effectiveness	Communication Mastery
Engagement	Dealing with the Speed of Life
The Art of Results	Time Effectiveness
Influence	Meeting Effectiveness

Keynote Speeches

Tony Jeary and Peter Thomas are available for keynote speaking, both separately and together.

•

**To discuss how we can bring value to you
and your organization, email us at info@tonyjeary.com
or call us at 817.430.9422.**

Appendix

Best Books That Have Impacted Our Lives (and Audio and Videos)

SPIRITUAL:

The Bible

30 Days to Understanding the Bible, Max Anders

A Life Well Spent, Russ Crosson

Halftime: Moving from Success to Significance, Bob P. Buford

The Man In The Mirror, Patrick Morley

ATTITUDE/MOTIVATION:

Charisma: Seven Keys to Developing the Magnetism That Leads to Success, Tony Alessandra

Do It! Let's Get Off Our Butts, Peter McWilliams

The Power Of Positive Thinking, Norman Vincent Peale

You 2: A High Velocity Formula for Multiplying Your Personal Effectiveness in Quantum Leaps by Price Pritchett

You Can't Afford the Luxury of a Negative Thought, Peter McWilliams

MARRIAGE:

1001 Ways to Be Romantic, Gregory Godek

Simple Secrets of a Wonderful Marriage

The Five Love Languages, Gary Chapman

PERSONAL IMPROVEMENT:
Strategic Acceleration: Succeed at the Speed of Life, Tony Jeary
Charisma: Seven Keys to Developing the Magnetism That Leads to Success, Tony Alessandra
Flow: The Psychology of Optimal Experience, Mihaly Csikszentmihalyi
How to Win Friends and Influence People, Dale Carnegie
The 7 Habits Of Highly Effective People, Stephen R. Covey
The Spellbinders Gift, Og Mandino

CHILDREN:
Positive Self-Talk For Children, Douglas Bloch
She Calls Me Daddy, Robert Wolgemuth

ORGANIZATION:
Breathing Space: Living and Working at a Comfortable Pace in a Sped-Up Society, Jeff Davison
Organizing Your Work Space, Odette Pollar
The Organized Executive, Stephanie Winston

WEALTH:
Don't Worry, Make Money, Richard Carlson
How To Think Like A Millionaire, Mark Fisher and Marc Allen
The Millionaire Next Door, Thomas Stanley and William Danko
Think and Grow Rich, Napoleon Hill

NEGOTIATING:
How To Argue And Win Every Time, Gerry Spence

MARKETING/PROMOTION:
Networking With The Affluent, Thomas Stanley
The Harvey MacKay Rolodex Network Builder, Harvey MacKay

BUSINESS IMPROVEMENT:
The One Minute Entrepreneur, Kenneth Blanchard
The One Minute Manager, Kenneth Blanchard and Spencer Johnson
The E-Myth Revisited, Michael Gerber
Let's Get Results, Not Excuses!, James M. Bleech and Dr. David Mutchler
Managing Transitions, William Bridges
The 80/20 Principle, Richard Koch
The Aladdin Factor, Jack Canfield
The Art of Being Well Informed, Andrew P. Garvin and Robert Berkman
We've Got to Stop Meeting Like This, Tony Jeary and George Lowe
The Ultimate Blueprint for an Insanely Successful Business, Keith Cunningham

CONSULTING:
Get Slightly Famous, Steven Van Yoder
How to be the Number One Authority in Your Market, Dave Newton
High Visibility, Irving Rein, Philip Kotler, Michael Hamlin and Martin Stoller

PRESENTING:
Inspire Any Audience, Tony Jeary and Zig Ziglar

SALES:
Selling to VITO the Very Important Top Officer, Anthony Parinello

SUCCESS:
Psychology of Success, Dennis Waitley
Be Great: The Five Foundations of an Extraordinary Life, Peter H. Thomas

PRESENTATION/MARKETING COLLATERAL AUDIT

ORGANIZATIONAL NAME: DATE:

#	Collateral Item (What)	Rating 1-10	Purpose (Notes)	Action (How)	Budget
1. Clarity					
1.	Branding Matrix				
2.	Strategic Business Plan				
3.	Logo*				
4.	Value Proposition or Unique Selling Position (USP)				
5.	Slogan/Jingle/Tagline*				
6.	Color Scheme*				
7.	Customer Focus				
8.	Organization's Profile				
9.	Message Matrix				
10.	Text Matrix				
11.	Competitive Comparison				
2. Base Communication					
12.	Stationery: Letterhead, Envelopes and Mailing Labels*				
13.	Fax Cover Sheet				
14.	Business Cards*				
15.	Christmas Cards				
16.	Zcard				
17.	Plastic Business Cards				
18.	Brochure(s)*				
19.	One sheets*				
20.	Press Kit				
21.	Newsletter				
22.	Business Reply Card				
23.	Direct Mail Pieces				
24.	Catalogs				
25.	Stationery: Thank You Cards				
26.	Personalized Index Cards				
27.	Forms				
28.	Self-Inking Stamps / Labels				
29.	Biography(ies)*				
30.	Pitch Book				
31.	Brag Book				
32.	Statement Stuffers				

#	Collateral Item (What)	Rating 1-10	Purpose (Notes)	Action (How)	Budget
33.	Exterior Signs				
34.	Vehicle Identification				
35.	Interior Signs				
36.	Foam Board				
	3. Electronic/Web				
37.	Website				
38.	Auto Responders				
39.	Social Media				
40.	Blogs				
41.	YouTube				
42.	YouTube Channel				
43.	E-mail Stationery (electronic letterhead):				
44.	PowerPoint Message				
45.	Video				
46.	Disc Brochures*				
47.	Disc Brochure Covers				
48.	Thumb Drives				
49.	Playaway				
50.	Telephone System Messages -- On Hold and Voice Mail				
51.	Software / Software Inserts				
52.	Media-Ready CD				
	4. Prospecting				
53.	Distributor Kit				
54.	DVD for Prospecting/Recruiting				
55.	CD for Prospecting/Recruiting				
56.	Product Brochures				
57.	Opportunity Brochures				
58.	Online Tools for Prospecting/Recruiting				
59.	Online Training				
60.	Magazines for Prospects/Recruits				
61.	Autoship programs for Tools				
	5. Resources and Archives				
62.	Photo Library				
63.	References/Testimonial Letters				
64.	Database				
65.	Database Software				
66.	Case Studies				

#	Collateral Item (What)	Rating 1-10	Purpose (Notes)	Action (How)	Budget
			6. Merchandising/Give-Aways		
67.	Trade Show Materials				
68.	Pop-Ups				
69.	Calculator				
70.	Legal Pads				
71.	Desk Trinkets				
72.	Luggage Tags				
73.	T-shirts				
74.	Hats				
75.	Posters				
76.	Banners and Signs				
77.	Bumper Stickers				
78.	Calendars				
79.	Envelope Teaser				
80.	Coupons/Tickets				
81.	Door Hangers				
82.	Point of Purchase Materials				
83.	Card Decks				
84.	Newspaper Inserts				
85.	Advertisement Templates (Icons)				
			7. Press and Community Relations		
86.	Articles and Columns Written				
87.	Reprints				
88.	Organizations and Affiliations				
89.	Organizations Started				
90.	Community Involvement				
91.	Marketing with Celebrities				
92.	Media Releases				
93.	Feature Stories				
94.	Guest on Talk Show or Radio				
95.	Awards Received				
96.	Awards Sponsored				
97.	Contests & Events Created				
98.	Contests & Events Sponsored				
99.	Celebrity Sponsor/Spokesperson				

#	Collateral Item (What)	Rating 1-10	Purpose (Notes)	Action (How)	Budget
			8. Publishing		
100.	Trophy Book				
101.	Handbook				
102.	Passport Book				
103.	White Paper				
104.	CD/DVD				
			9. Events and Training		
105.	Tent Cards				
106.	Action Cards				
107.	Notetakers/Handouts				
108.	Coined Phrases				
109.	Coaching Cards				
110.	Bio Cards				
111.	Evaluations				
112.	Special-Titled Processes				
113.	Pre-Session Survey				
114.	Event Check List				
115.	Signatures (dollar bill pads)				
116.	Follow-up				
117.	Lunch and Learn Kits				
118.	Cascade Kits				
			10. Institutional Advertising		
119.	Classified Ads				
120.	Yellow Pages				
			11. Internal Marketing		
121.	Badge Backer				
122.	Scorecard				
123.	Storyboard				
			Other		
124.	Strategic Studio				
125.	War Room				

Tammy Kling about to board

Tammy, Tony, Peter and Rita, celebration lunch, Victoria Canada

Peter and Tony, off the Thomas Spirit for a walk discussing this book

A Final Thought

The 12 Traits of the
Renaissance Man or Woman

I am outstanding in my field and exceptional in many areas.
I am insatiably curious.
I embrace culture.
I merge my left brain and my right brain.
I delight in sharing what I do.
I have the courage to take risks.
I create.
I persevere.
I am passionate.
I have vision.
I challenge the status quo.
I shape the future.
I am a Renaissance man or woman.

Notes